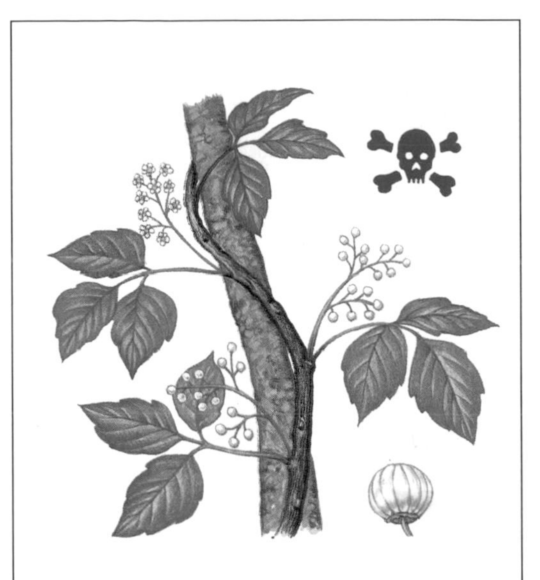

Poison Ivy and Poison Oak

This weed (above) causes an itchy rash if you touch it. Poison Ivy grows like a vine, and Poison Oak grows like a shrub. Try to remember what the leaves look like, and do not touch it. If you do touch it, washing your hands as soon as possible may reduce the itching. Your local drug store will have various remedies that will help.

Bird Size Scale

One of these symbols are shown beside each bird. They show you at a glance how big the bird is likely to be. All measurements describe the length of the bird from its beak-tip to the end of its tail feathers. In this example the bird will be between 7 and 10 inches long.

SCIENCE NATURE GUIDES

BIRDS
OF NORTH AMERICA

EDITED BY
Angela Royston

US CONSULTANT
Paul Baicich

Conservation

As a bird-watcher you must play your part in protecting wildlife and the countryside. To make sure you do not harm the birds or other wildlife, read and follow the Bird-watcher's Code below. Don't forget that it is against the law to collect feathers, eggs, or nests throughout the US today.

Plants, birds, insects, and other animals live together in a complex pattern of relationships. Be careful not to disturb the smaller habitats (like a forest or a field) you are walking through by damaging plants or frightening birds unnecessarily.

Visit your local bird sanctuaries. You can enjoy seeing the birds, but you can also see what is being done to help them. On page 78, you will find the names of some organizations who campaign for the preservation of birds and their environments. By joining them and supporting their efforts, you can help to preserve our birds for the future.

Bird-watcher's Code

1. **Observe and photograph birds** without disturbing them wherever possible.
2. **Keep a good distance** from nests and nesting colonies.
3. **Leave birds in peace.** Don't chase them or make them fly unnecessarily.
4. **Don't touch or pick up fledglings and eggs**. If you do, the parents may abandon them and they will die.
5. **Keep to existing roads, trails and pathways** wherever possible.
6. **Keep off private property** unless you already have permission to go on it.
7. **Leave all gates as you find them.**

Thunder Bay Press
5880 Oberlin Drive
Suite 400
San Diego, CA 92121

First published in the United States
by Thunder Bay Press, 1994

Complete Cataloging in Publication (CIP) is available
through the Library of Congress.
LC Card Number: 93-48675

Edited text and captions by Angela Royston, based on *Birds of North America* by Frank Shaw, published by Dragon's World.

Species illustrations by Norman Arlott, Trevor Boyer, Malcolm Ellis, Robert Morton, Maurice Pledger, Christopher Rose and David Thelwell, all of Bernard Thornton Artists, London.
Habitat paintings and headbands by Antonia Phillips.
Identification and activities illustrations by Richard Coombes.

Editor Diana Briscoe
Designer James Lawrence
Design Assistant Victoria Furbisher
Editorial Director Pippa Rubinstein

Printed in Spain

ISBN 1 85028 261 7

Contents

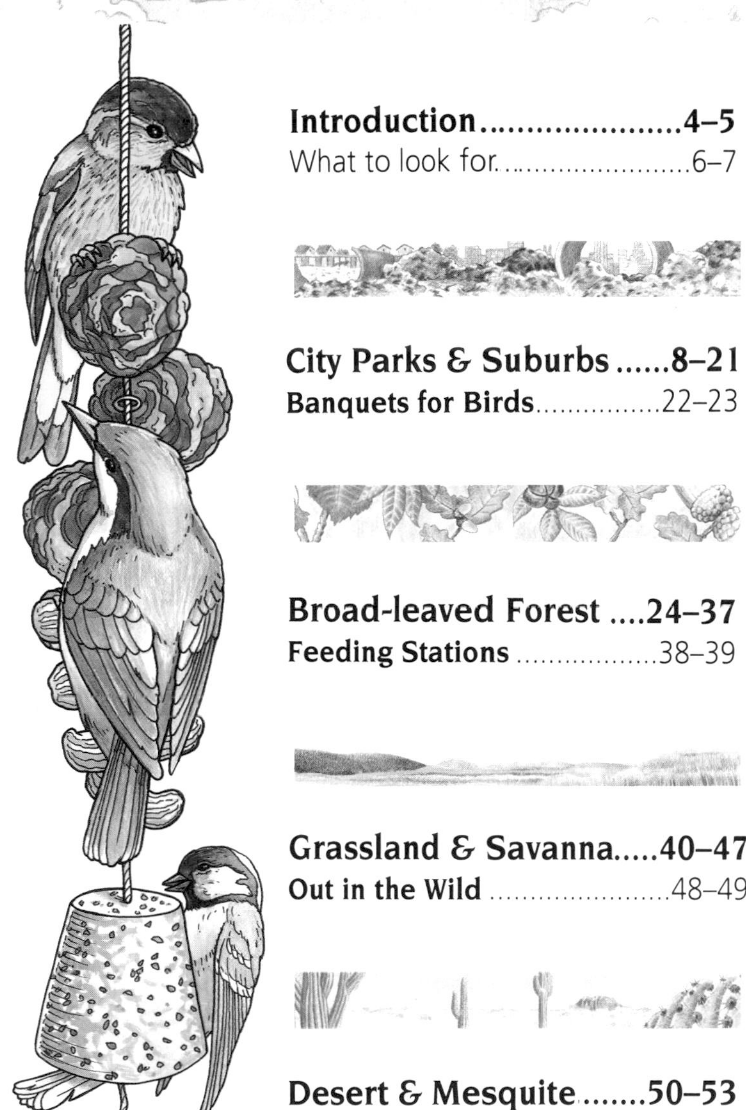

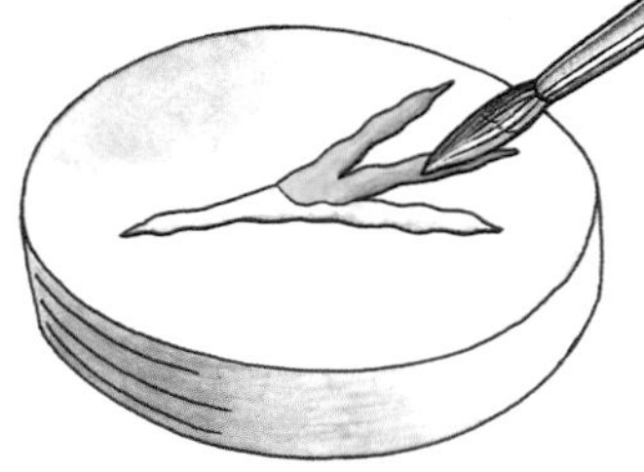

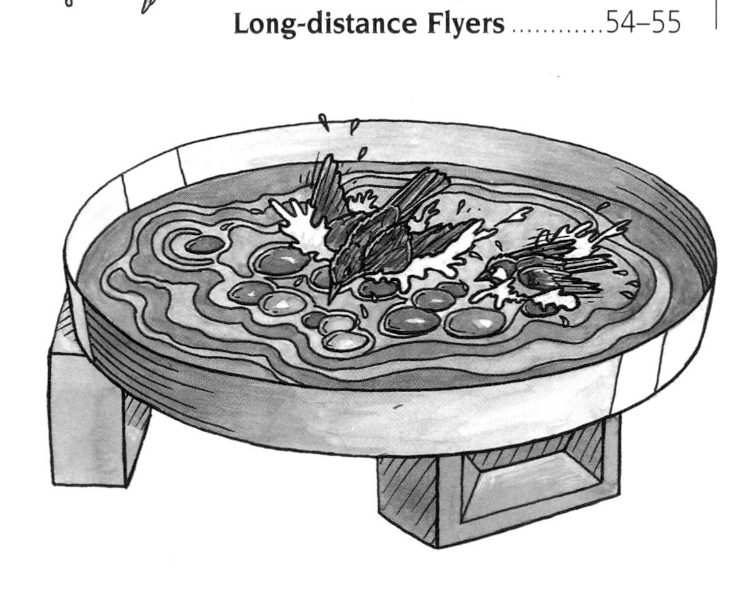

Birds Are Everywhere

About 645 different types of birds breed in North America, but many other kinds —over 200 species—visit here as well. If you are not an expert bird-watcher, trying to identify one bird among so many can be hard to do.

If you really want to get to know birds and where to see them, you have to be a naturalist, not just a bird-watcher. Birds rely on their surroundings for food, places to roost (sleep), and good nesting sites, and these vary from habitat to habitat. When you know what a habitat provides, you will know what birds you might expect to see there.

This book will make this job easier for you in two ways. It shows you only the birds you are most likely to see, and it puts them in groups according to the habitat, or kind of countryside, where you are most likely to see them.

So, don't look for a Red-throated Loon in the prairies or a Wood Thrush by the sea. They know where they are most likely to find the food they eat and, with practice, so will you.

From egg to bird

You will see birds at all stages of their lives, if you watch birds regularly. But don't expect any particular bird always to look just like the picture in this book. Its color and markings may be different if it is a female or a young bird. Males are usually the most brightly colored of the two. Their markings show best during the breeding season when they are trying to attract the females.

How to use this book

To identify a bird you don't recognize, like the hawk and the sparrow shown above, follow these steps.

1 **Draw a field sketch** quickly as shown on page 49. First make sure of its size and shape. Then look for any special features (pages 6–7 show you the kind of things you should look for.)

2 **Decide what habitat you are in**. If you aren't sure, read the descriptions at the start of each section to see which one fits best. Each habitat has a different picture band heading and these are shown below.

3 **Look through the pages of birds** with this picture band. The picture and information given for each bird will help you to identify it. The large bird (left) is a Sharp-shinned Hawk (see page 30.)

4 **If you can't find the bird there**, look through the other sections. Birds move round and you will surely see many of them in more than one habitat. You will find the small bird (left) is a White-throated Sparrow (see page 17.)

5 **If you still can't find the bird**, you may have to look in a larger field guide (see page 78 for some suggestions.) You might have spotted a very rare bird!

Top-of-page Picture Bands

This book is divided into different habitats. Each habitat (type of countryside) has a different picture band at the top of the page. These are shown below.

Desert & Mesquite

City Parks & Suburbs

Broad-leaved Forest

Grassland & Savanna

Evergreen Forest

Seashores & Marshes

Rivers, Lakes & Marshes

Parts of a bird

When you are trying to identify a bird, look for patches of color and stripes on its wings, tail, and body. Is the color of its back different to its chest or belly? Does it have eye stripes or chin stripes? Look for bands on the wings or tail. The text for each bird tells you the colors and markings you are most likely to see.

Bills or beaks

The shape of a bird's bill depends on the kind of food that it eats.

A wader has a long, thin, curved bill for catching insects.

A heron is a wading bird. It uses its very long bill to stab fish in shallow water.

A hawk has a sharp, hooked bill for tearing meat.

A duck has a flat bill for dabbling in water to sift for tiny creatures.

A finch has a short, stout bill for cracking seeds.

Wing shapes

When a bird is flying, look at the shape of its wings and the pattern of its flight.

A finch has short, broad wings for flitting from tree to tree.

A swift has narrow, swept-back wings for flying fast through the air.

An eagle has long, broad wings for soaring and hovering.

A seagull has straight, narrow wings for soaring and gliding over the sea.

Feet and legs

The shape of a bird's feet and legs are made for the way it lives.

Hawks and other birds of prey use their sharp talons for grasping their prey.

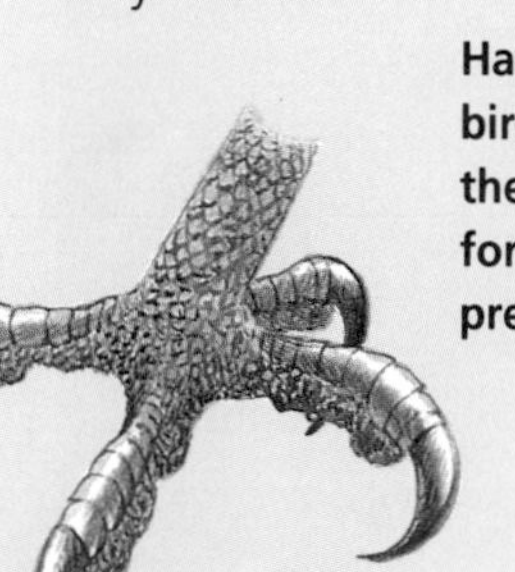

Tree-climbers like woodpeckers use their long toes and claws to grip the tree trunk.

Waterbirds, like ducks, have webbed feet for paddling through water.

Ground birds, like pheasants, have strong, thick toes to scratch with.

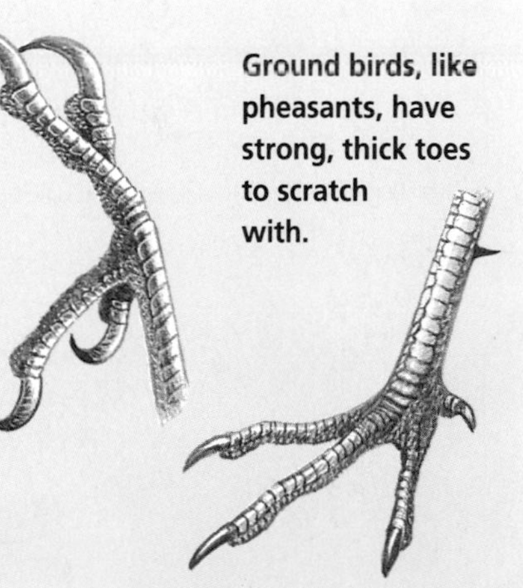

City Parks & Suburbs

You may think that the busy streets, skyscrapers, and paved areas of city centers and towns would be unsuitable for birds, but not only pigeons, sparrows and starlings come here. Parks provide islands of trees and grass in the sprawling concrete of cities. Suburban yards form large areas of varied shrubs and trees. They provide food and nesting sites for many different kinds of birds.

So many birds have learned to take advantage of buildings and human habitation that you could wonder how some managed before the early settlers arrived. But, of course, Chimney Swifts did manage without chimneys, Barn Swallows without buildings, and American Robins without lawns.

Although the birds in this section are well adapted to living near people you can see them in many other habitats, too. Between the suburbs and rural woodland, you often find semi-open country with scattered trees and bushes, and thickets, that attracts several kinds of wilder birds.

You too can encourage birds to come into your yard. The activities pages in this book will give you some ideas, but make sure that any birds that come to feed or nest are safe from cats. The picture shows nine birds from this book; how many can you recognize?

Indigo Bunting, Northern Cardinal, Black-capped Chickadee, Blue Jay, American Robin, Chipping Sparrow, Barn Swallow, Downy Woodpecker, House Wren

Eastern & Western Screech-Owls

These small owls may be mainly rusty colored or gray. They have large yellow eyes and ear tufts that stand out clearly when raised. They hunt at night, their fluffy feathers letting them fly very quietly. Listen for their different calls—a quavering whinny in the Eastern and a series of accelerating whistles in the Western. They like woods, orchards, and parks, and build their nests in tree holes or woodpecker holes. They will also use birdhouses. The females lay 4 or 5 white eggs which are incubated as soon as they are laid so the eggs hatch at different times.

Family Group: Owl
Size: 8–9 ins
Usually hunts alone
Eats insects and small animals

Northern Oriole

This bird is usually seen in the summer in suburban trees. The male is easy to see with its black head, back, and breast, and bright orange underparts and rump. (The western variety has an orange cheek and eyebrow.) Look for the patch or stripe of white on its black wings. The female is brownish on top and warm orange below. Orioles love to sing, so listen for its fluty whistles. Its nest is a neat pouch of grasses hung high in a tree. The female lays 3 to 6 white eggs spotted with brown.

Family Group: Oriole
Size: 8–9 ins
Alone or in pairs
Eats insects and berries
Summer visitor

Barn Owl

This ghost-like owl has a white breast and face and cinnamon upper parts. It hunts mainly at dawn and dusk. Although it can see very well at night, it also relies on its excellent sense of hearing to help it find its prey. Its usual call is a raspy hissing screech. It breeds in old buildings, barns, or broken trees. It nests in holes in trees or barns or in nest boxes where the female lays 4 to 7 white eggs.

Family Group: Owl
Size: 13–14 ins
Usually hunts alone
Eats rodents and other small creatures

Rufous Hummingbird

You will recognize these birds as hummingbirds because they hover at flowers to sip the nectar with their long beaks. You will see the Rufous Hummingbird only in the western parts of North America. The male Rufous Hummingbird has a reddish body, green wings, and a ruby-colored throat. The female has a green back and only ruby spots on her throat. She lays 2 white eggs.

Family Group: Hummingbird
Size: 3–4 ins
Usually feeds alone
Eats nectar of flowers
Summer visitor

Blue Jay

Family Group: Jay
Size: 10–11 ins
Usually alone or in pairs
Eats nuts, berries, insects and seeds
Also found in broad-leaved woods

This noisy, flashy bird is common in the eastern US and may be seen in even the largest cities. It is easy to see with its blue upper parts and distinctive blue crest. Look for the white bands across its wings and long tail striped with black. You will easily hear its call, a loud piercing JAY-JAY. It usually makes its nest in an evergreen tree and lays 4 to 6 greenish tan eggs spotted with brown.

Ruby-throated Hummingbird

Family Group: Hummingbird
Size: 3–4 ins
Usually feeds alone
Eats nectar of flowers
Summer visitor

You will recognize them as hummingbirds because they hover at flowers to sip the nectar with their long beaks. You will see the Ruby-throated Hummingbird only in the eastern US and southern Canada. The Ruby-throated Hummingbird is green on top and white underneath. The male has a ruby-colored throat patch which may look black in weak light. The female lays 2 white eggs.

Cedar Waxwing

There are two species of Waxwing in North America. Both have sleek crests and yellow-tipped tails, but the Cedar Waxwing is common all over North America and is the one you are most likely to see. It roams in huge flocks along hedgerows and in yards and can quickly eat all the berries off a bush. In fact, they will eat so many overripe berries that you may see them lying around on branches or the lawn, hardly able to fly. They nest in trees and the female lays 3 to 5 pale greenish blue eggs, spotted with black.

Family Group: Waxwing
Size: 6–7 ins
Forms noisy flocks
Eats berries

Chimney Swift

Swifts fly very fast and spend most of the day in the air. Their long, pointed wings and rounded, streamlined bodies are perfect for flying. They feed, drink, mate, gather twigs for their nests, and even wash themselves while flying. The Chimney Swift is common in North America east of the Rockies and is the only type of swift you are likely to see there. It twitters as it flies and looks like it doesn't have a tail. It nests in chimneys, gluing its nest to the side of the chimney with saliva. The female lays 4 or 5 white eggs.

Family Group: Swift
Size: 4–5 ins
Usually in groups
Eats flying insects
Summer visitor

Purple Martin

This chunky deep purple swallow has broader wings than other swallows. Look for its V-notched tail and the swallow-like way it flies—a short glide followed by rapid flapping, then another short glide. They used to nest in holes in trees or cliffs, but now often take advantage of bird apartment houses which are built for them. The females lay 4 or 5 white eggs and incubate them on their own.

Family Group: Swallow
Size: 7–8 ins
Usually in large flocks
Eats flying insects
Summer visitor

Northern Flicker

Woodpeckers are excellent tree-climbers. They have strong claws for clinging onto the bark and sharp beaks which they use like chisels to cut into the tree. They use their long, bristly tongues to catch the insects inside. The Northern Flicker also likes to feed on ants on the ground. It has brown wings and back, and a white rump and underparts, all spotted with black. Its underwing may flash yellow (in the East) or orange-pink (in the West). They drill a hole in a tree or pole to make a nest where the female lays 6 to 9 white eggs.

Family Group: Woodpecker
Size: 12–13 ins
Usually alone, though they may migrate in small groups
Eats insects that dig into trees

Barn Swallow

Swallows look very similar to swifts and, like them, love to fly. You can tell them apart because swifts fly with their wings bent closer to their bodies. The Barn Swallow is blue-black on top and rusty underneath. Look for its deeply forked tail. In the fall watch them gather in flocks on telephone wires before migrating southward. They breed over most of North America. They nest in barns and buildings and lay 4 or 5 white eggs, lightly spotted with red.

Family Group: Swallow
Size: 6–7 ins
Usually in flocks
Eats flying insects
Summer visitor

Downy Woodpecker

This small woodpecker has a white back, striped wings and white underparts. You can tell it apart from similar woodpeckers by its tiny beak. You are likely to see it in most of North America, clinging to the bark of a tree and boring into it in search of food. Watch for it on suburban birdfeeders, too. It makes its nest by digging a hole in a dead tree. The female lays 4 or 5 white eggs.

Family Group: Woodpecker
Size: 6–7 ins
Usually alone, or in pairs
Eats insects in tree bark
Also found in broad-leaved or evergreen woods

House Wren

In the spring and summer this little brown bird is common around houses and yards all across the US and southern Canada. Look for its chunky shape and short cocked tail. Wrens like to hide under thick plants and shrubs, but may perch in the open to sing. Listen for the House Wren's loud bubbly song. It nests in a hole in a building, bird house, a car, or even in a shoe or the pocket of a jacket. The female lays 6 to 8 pale pink eggs, spotted with reddish brown. In the fall it migrates south to the Gulf Coast and Mexico.

Family Group: Wren
Size: 4–5 ins
Usually alone
Eats insects, spiders, and their eggs

Common Grackle

The male is black with pale yellow eyes. The female is duller with brown eyes. In both look for the longish V-shaped tail. If you can get close to the male you may notice that his head and wings have a purplish gloss, and northern and western birds may have a bronze gloss on the breast and back. They breed in trees in parks and woods. Their nest is made of twigs and grasses bound with mud and the female lays 4 to 6 pale blue eggs spotted with brown.

Family Group: Blackbird
Size: 12½–14 ins
Forms large flocks
Eats insects, grains, small animals, and berries
Also found in fields and marshes
Summer visitor in the North and West

American Crow

This large, aggressive, black bird is hard to miss. It lives in groups and its call is the familiar CAW-CAW. Look for its powerful beak and, if it is flying, for its square-shaped tail. It is the largest crow and the one you are most likely to see in most parts of North America. It has adapted well to living near people. It makes its nest in a tree and builds a cup of twigs lined with any softer materials it can find. The female lays 4 to 6 greenish eggs blotched with brown.

Family Group: Crow
Size: 16–18 ins
Usually found in groups
Varied diet includes insects, fruit, eggs of other species
Also found in many other habitats

Gray Catbird

This bird is slate-gray with a black cap and black tail that it often holds straight up. It is usually seen east of the Rockies. It likes to hide in dense thickets, so listen for its call. You cannot mistake its cat-like whining, and its song includes many mews, too. Its large bulky nest is made of twigs lined with grasses and roots, in which the female lays 3 to 5 greenish blue eggs. It migrates to the Gulf and Atlantic coasts for the winter.

Family Group: Thrasher
Size: 8–9 ins
Usually in ones or twos
Eats insects, seeds, and berries
Also found in broad-leaved woods

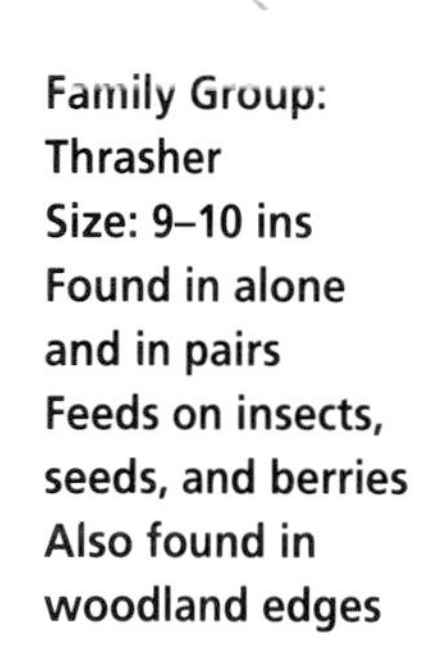

European Starling

This is another aggressive bird that is hard to miss with its shiny black plumage and yellow beak. It was brought over from Europe in 1890 and is now a pest almost everywhere. Watch it take over at birdfeeders. In the summer its back has an iridescent green and purple sheen. In the winter it is heavily spotted all over with white and tan. Listen for its twittering, particularly at dusk. It will also imitate the call of other birds. It builds its nest in any hole it can find in a tree or building. The female lays 5 to 7 pale blue eggs there.

Family Group: Starling
Size: 8–9 ins
Usually in large groups
Eats insects, worms, fruit, and seeds

Northern Mockingbird

The Northern Mockingbird is dull gray on top, paler underneath. It has dark gray wings and tail. Look for the white outer tail-feathers and patches of white when it is flying or preening itself. It is best known for its songs and may be heard singing from rooftops and television antennas until long after dark. It will mimic other birds' songs, even squeaky gates, barking dogs, and pianos. In the spring the male may sing for hours, both day and night. It nests in a tree and the female lays 4 or 5 bluish eggs spotted with brown.

Family Group: Thrasher
Size: 9–10 ins
Found in alone and in pairs
Feeds on insects, seeds, and berries
Also found in woodland edges

American Robin

You can easily tell this well-known bird by its rich red-orange underparts and brown upper parts. Look for its streaked white bib and white lower belly. You may see it standing on the lawn with its head cocked to one side, looking for earthworms. It has a loud, melodic warble which sounds like CHEERILY, CHEER-UP, CHEERIO. Its nest is a neat cup of grasses and mud in which the female lays 3 to 5 pale blue eggs.

Family Group: Thrush
Size: 9–10 ins
Alone or in groups, flocking especially during migration
Eats earthworms, insects, berries

House Sparrow

Although this bird looks like the American sparrows, it has shorter legs and a thicker beak. Since it was brought here from Europe in 1850 it has become established wherever people live. The male is streaked black and chestnut on top and dirty gray-cream underneath. Look for his white cheeks and black bib. The female is dully colored with a streaked back. She nests in holes in buildings in cities and farms and lays three broods of 3 to 5 gray eggs blotched with darker gray.

Family Group: Weaver Finch
Size: 6–7 ins
Usually in groups
Eats seeds and food left-overs

Chipping Sparrow

Sparrows are often difficult to tell apart since they are all streaked brown and tan on top with paler underparts. But, when it is breeding, you can tell the Chipping Sparrow by its chestnut crown, white stripe above its eyes and black stripe through its eyes. Its call is a trilling CHIP-CHIP-CHIP and in the summer you are likely to see it feeding on lawns. It nests in trees where the female lays 3 to 5 blue eggs speckled with brown.

Family Group: Sparrow
Size: 5–6 ins
Usually in pairs or small groups
Eats seeds
Also found in many other habitats

White-throated Sparrow

You are most likely to see this sparrow visiting a birdfeeder or hunched up on the ground. Look for the bold stripes on its head and for its white bib and rich chestnut upper parts. It breeds in much of Canada and the northeastern US. It nests on the ground under a bush and lays 3 to 5 pale gray eggs, spotted with green or brown. In the fall you may see it migrating south, mainly to the lowlands of the eastern and southern US, but also to the coast of California.

Family Group: Bunting and Sparrow
Size: 6–7 ins
Usually in groups
Eats insects and seeds

Northern Cardinal

This is one of the easiest birds to identify with its bright red crest and plumage. Look for its black face and pink beak. The female is tannish-brown with red on her wings, crest, and tail. Listen for its song—a loud ringing whistle with many variations. This is a tolerant bird that has learned to live successfully alongside people. Its nest is made of twigs and grasses. The female usually incubates the 3 or 4 white eggs spotted with brown on her own.

Family Group: Bunting and Sparrow
Size: 8–9 ins
Usually in pairs
Eats seeds
Also found in woodland edges and marshes

Song Sparrow

Most sparrows have strong feet for perching on twigs and branches, and short beaks. Watch them flit from perch to perch. Look for the Song Sparrow's long rounded tail, which tells it apart from other sparrows. Look at the streaking on its breast which usually leads to a central solid spot. Its song is 3 or 4 clear notes followed by a trill. It nests on the ground, building a cup of grasses in which the female lays 3 to 5 blue-green eggs spotted with brown.

Family Group: Sparrow
Size: 6–7 ins
Usually in pairs or small groups
Eats seeds

House Finch

The male is brown with a red breast and red band over his forehead and eyes. His underparts are tan streaked with brown, unlike the larger American Robin. The female is brownish, streaked with dark brown on top and bottom. They nest in holes in trees and buildings, in nest boxes, and in the old nests of other birds. Their 4 or 5 blue eggs are spotted with black.

Family Group: Finch
Size: 5–6 ins
Usually in flocks
Eats seeds
Also found in dry grasslands

Common Yellowthroat

This bird is olive on top and yellow underneath. Look for the male's black face mask. It is common and widespread, but spends much of its time living in low shrubs and plants. If you see it, its tail could be standing straight up like a wren's. Listen for its song, a repeated WITCHITY. It nests on the ground all across North America. Its nest is made of stems and grass in which the female lays 3 to 5 white eggs, spotted with brown. It is a summer visitor to all but the far South and coastal states.

Family Group: Wood Warbler
Size: 5–6 ins
Alone or in pairs
Eats insects
Also found in freshwater marshes

Yellow Warbler

The Yellow Warbler is probably the most common of these small brightly colored birds. The male's yellow plumage and chestnut streaking on his breast makes him easy to see, especially in the spring. In the fall he looks more like the female, paler and greener. Listen for its clear song—SWEET SWEET I'M SO SWEET. It breeds in damp thickets and builds its nest with whatever it can find including pieces of string and twine. The female lays 4 or 5 white eggs, often with a wash of blue, and speckled with brown.

Family Group: Wood Warbler
Size: 5–6 ins
Alone or in pairs
Eats insects
Summer visitor

Yellow-breasted Chat

This is our largest warbler and is found over most of the US. It is brown on top and yellow underneath. It is a shy bird and spends most of the time hiding in dense thickets and bushes. The male often sings from an open perch, or hovers to preen himself in spring. Look for the small black mask and white on his face and the short chunky beak. You may hear its chattering song even at night. It makes its nest of leaves and grass where the female lays 3 to 5 white eggs spotted with brown.

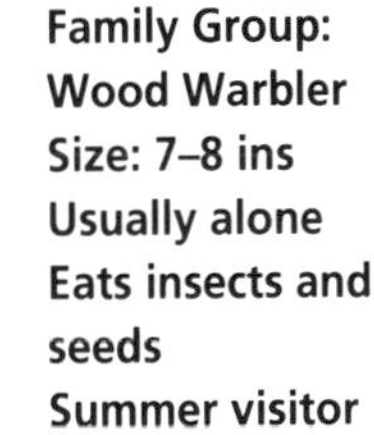

Family Group: Wood Warbler
Size: 7–8 ins
Usually alone
Eats insects and seeds
Summer visitor

Indigo Bunting

This bunting is found only in the East. The male is the only finch which is blue all over, but in weak light it might look black. The female is streaked rusty-brown above, and tannish below with indistinct streaks. You may hear the male singing his warbled song long into August. The nest is a cup of twigs and grasses which they make in a bush. The female lays 3 or 4 white eggs washed with blue.

Family Group: Bunting and Sparrow
Size: 5–6 ins – Alone or in pairs
Eats seeds, insects, and berries – Summer visitor
Also found on edges of woods and thickets

Lazuli Bunting

This bunting is found only in western states. The male is blue on top and on his neck. His breast and sides are cinnamon and his belly is white. Look for the two white bands on his wings. The female is grayish brown with paler bands on her wings. The song is a rising and falling warble with repeated phrases in the opening notes. They nest in bushes, laying 3 or 4 white eggs washed with blue.

Family Group: Finch – Size: 5–6 ins
Alone or in groups – Eats seeds
Also found in woods and dense growth of shrubs or trees
Summer visitor to the western US

Rock Dove

City pigeons vary in color and markings, but they are easy to recognize from their plump bodies and small heads. You will also recognize their familiar OOO-ROO-COO call. Some pigeons are kept for racing because of their great "homing" instinct, and they were used in wartime to carry messages, even during World War II. They feed during the day in parks and fields. At night they roost on high window ledges, bridges, and barns. They nest in holes in buildings and lay 2 pure white eggs.

Family Group: Pigeon
Size: 11–13 ins
Usually in flocks
Eats grains, seeds, and fruit

Mourning Dove

This trim-shaped pigeon has brown upper parts spotted with black and a rich pinkish breast. When it is flying it looks dark all over, so look then for its long tail tapering to a point. Listen for its call—a mournful OOOH-OO-OO-OO—and the fluttering whistle its wings make as it takes off. Its nest is a platform of twigs built in a tree in which the female lays 2 white eggs. It has a very long breeding season and usually has 3 or 4 broods each year.

Family Group: Pigeon
Size: 11–12 ins
Often in flocks
Eats grains, seeds, and fruit
Also found on farms and fields

Family Group: Chickadee and Titmouse
Size: 4–5 ins
Often flock together, especially in the winter
Eats insects, seeds, and berries
Also found in broad-leaved and evergreen woods

Black-capped Chickadee

This small gray bird is easy to spot from its black cap and bib and white cheeks. You may see it searching for food among the leaves and bark of trees or, if you put out a birdfeeder, you will probably find it is the first to arrive. Listen for it calling CHICK-DEE-DEE-DEE. You may see it in most of North America except the southern states. It makes its nest in a hole in a rotten tree stump and lays 6 to 8 white eggs, spotted with reddish brown.

Family Group: Chickadee and Titmouse
Size: 6–7 ins
Often flock together
Eats insects, seeds, and berries

Tufted Titmouse

This titmouse is gray on top and white underneath with a wash of warm brownish red on its sides. Look for the dark gray crest and black forehead. This bird is common in the eastern US although there are some in southern Texas which have black crests. You will find them eager to eat from birdfeeders. Listen for its song, a repeated PEETA, PEETA, PEETA. The female lays 5 or 6 white eggs, lightly speckled with brown.

Plain Titmouse

Titmice have short beaks, short wings, and small crests. You may see them hanging upside down from twigs while they eat. The Plain Titmouse is named well, because it is gray on top and paler gray underneath with no other field marks to look for. Its call is a harsh SIC-A-DEE-DEE. You may see it only in the Southwest from California to Colorado. It makes its nest in a hole in a tree, building or post, and lays 5 to 8 white eggs, lightly spotted with brown.

Family Group: Chickadee and Titmouse
Size: 5–6 ins
Often flock together
Eats insects, seeds, and berries
Also found in woods

Eastern Phoebe

Tyrant Flycatchers are often difficult to tell apart. This one is brown on top and white underneath, although in the fall its belly looks yellowish. You can recognize it best from its song—a harsh FEE-BE. Look for it perched on a branch and fluffing its feathers and spreading its tail. Wait for it to dart out after flying insects. It breeds in much of North America except on the West Coast. It often nests under bridges and lays 5 white eggs, sometimes spotted. It migrates to the Gulf and Atlantic coasts for the winter.

Family Group: Tyrant Flycatcher
Size: 6–7 ins
Alone or in pairs
Eats flying insects
Also found in woods and on farms

Carolina Chickadee

This bird looks a lot like the Black-capped Chickadee but is found only in the southeastern US. In some places, like the Appalachians, you may see both birds but the Black-capped usually keeps to higher ground. To tell them apart, listen for their songs. The Carolina Chickadee's is a high-pitched fast FEE-BEE or FEE-BEE-EE. Its CHICKA-DEE call is faster. Like the Black-capped, they nest in holes in dead trees and lay 6 to 8 white eggs, speckled with reddish brown.

Family Group: Chickadee and Titmouse
Size: 4–5 ins
Often flock together
Eats insects, seeds, and berries
Also found in broad-leaved and evergreen woods

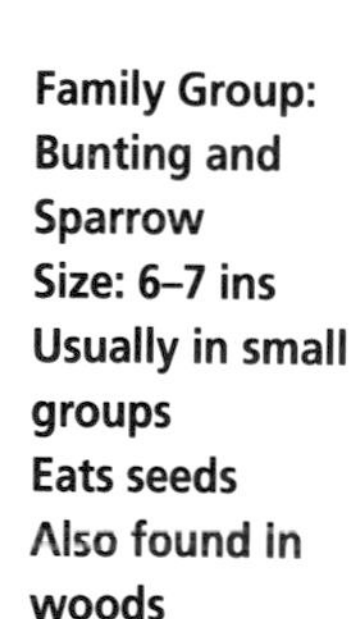

Dark-eyed Junco

Family Group: Bunting and Sparrow
Size: 6–7 ins
Usually in small groups
Eats seeds
Also found in woods

You are sure to see this bird at some time of the year all over North America. It is a common visitor to birdfeeders. Look for it in the spring in the far North and in the winter in the South. It is usually gray or brown on top and on the chest with a white belly, but some birds vary in color on their head, back, and belly. Look for the white on each side of its tail when it is flying. The female lays 4 to 6 white eggs spotted with brown.

Banquets for Birds

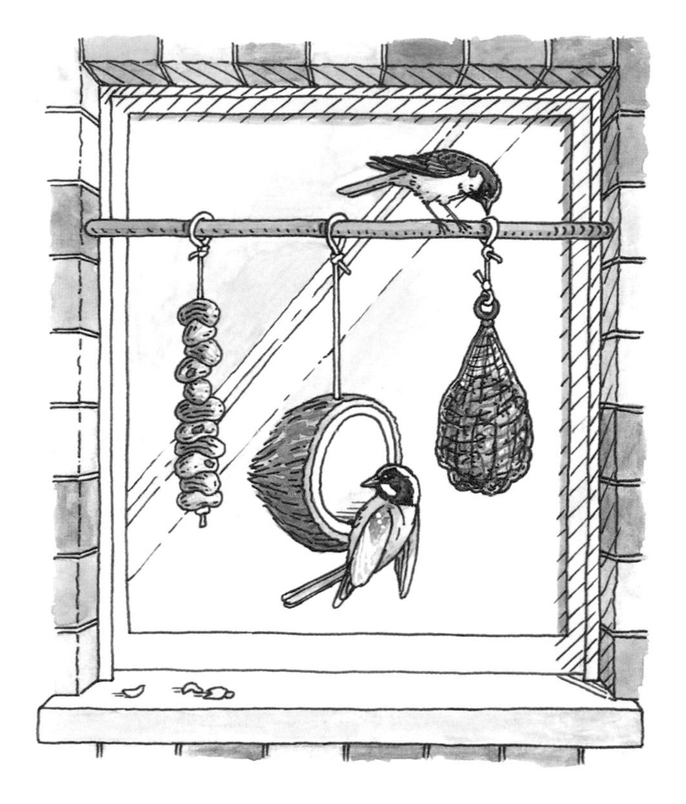

Different birds like to feed in different ways. Some like to feed on the ground, so all you have to do for them is to scatter some food there. Others, like warblers and tohees, feed on the seeds of trees and bushes. They are most likely to visit your garden if you hang pine cones and other food from your feeder. Here are some ideas for feeding them.

If you live in an apartment and do not have a back yard, you can still make a small feeding station by fixing a strong pole across a window and hanging food from it. There are plenty of birds in even the busiest cities and they will soon get used to you watching them if you keep very still.

Seeds

You can buy "Wild Bird Seed" or "Chick Scratch" from your supermarket or pet store, but check that it contains grit. Other seeds that birds like include sunflower, millet and hemp seeds, and corn.

Don't feed the bird seed sold for cage birds to wild birds because it does not contain the right mixture of seeds.

Coconuts

Ask an adult to help you to drill through one of the eyes of the coconut and drain off the milk. Then ask them to saw a section off the other end (about a quarter of its length). Drill another hole through the second eye and thread some wire or plastic string through the holes so that you can hang it up from a branch or the edge of a feeding station.

Scraps

Bacon rind, fruit like apple cores or orange segments, shelled unsalted peanuts, and water-soaked raisins are all good food for birds.

Beware of giving them too many bread or cake crumbs because these fill the bird's stomach without giving it the energy it needs.

Peanut chains

Buy some raw peanuts in their shells. Get some thin wire and string peanuts onto it by pushing the wire through the middle of the shell. Put about 10–12 nuts on each wire and hang them up from a branch or the edge of a feeding station.

Alternatively, you can tie the peanuts into a row with a string around their middles. These nuts may also attract squirrels.

Pine cone feeders

1 **Collect seven or eight pine cones** (the short, squat sort work best).

2 **Ask an adult to melt 2 oz of lard** in a pan and set it aside to cool.

3 **Stir in 1 oz of all-natural peanut butter** plus a large tablespoon of flour or cornmeal. (The flour is important because it soaks up the grease from the peanut butter.)

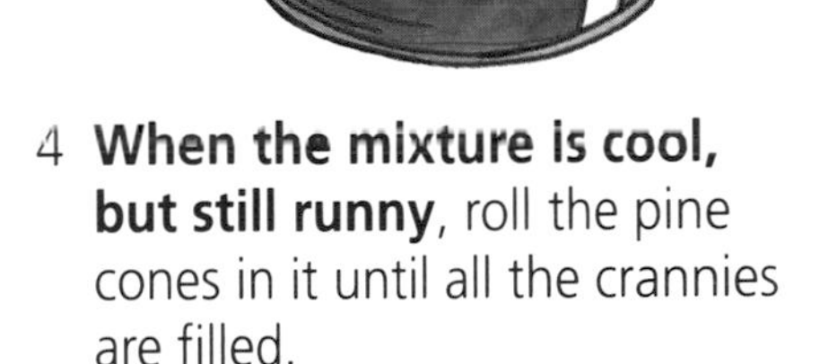

4 **When the mixture is cool, but still runny**, roll the pine cones in it until all the crannies are filled.

5 **Screw an eye-screw into the stem** of each pine cone, and then use a wire or some string to hang them up from a branch or the edge of a feeding station. These pine cones can be refilled when the birds have eaten the lard.

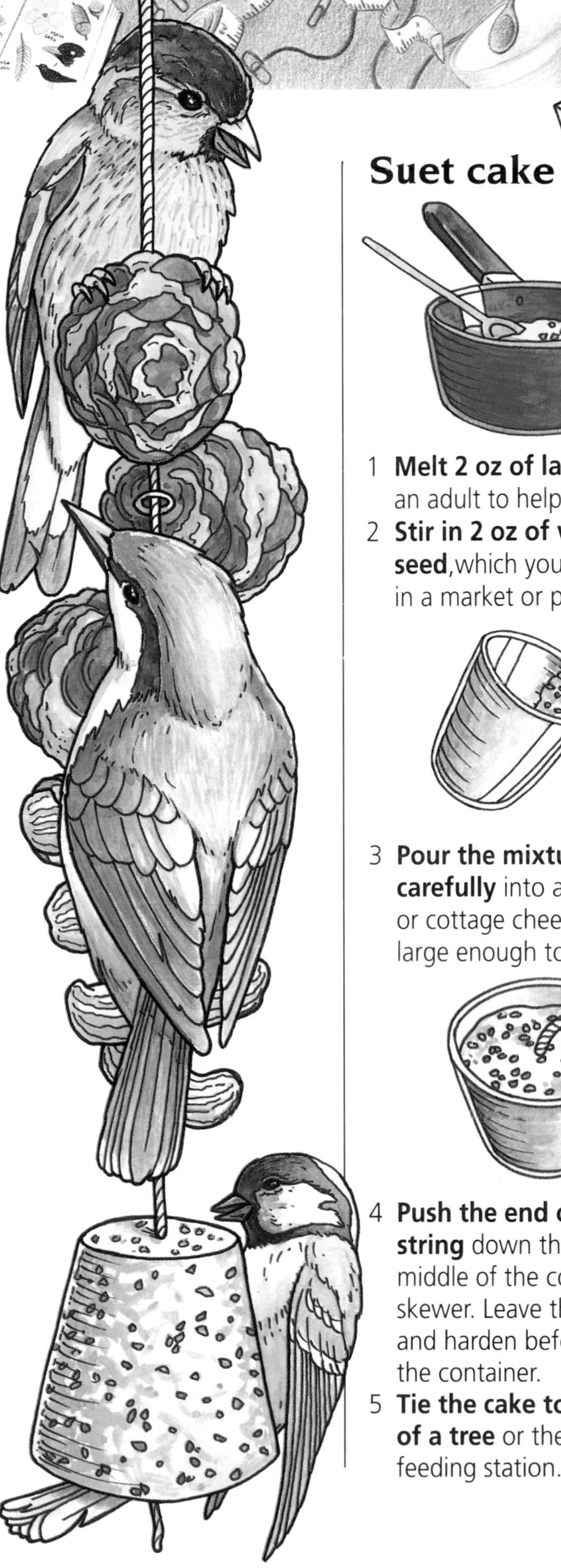

Suet cake

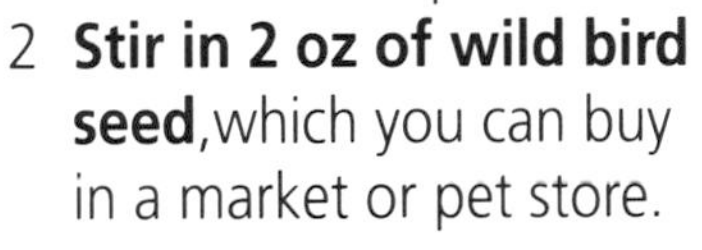

1 **Melt 2 oz of lard** in a pan. Ask an adult to help.

2 **Stir in 2 oz of wild bird seed**,which you can buy in a market or pet store.

3 **Pour the mixture very carefully** into a plastic yogurt or cottage cheese container, large enough to hold it.

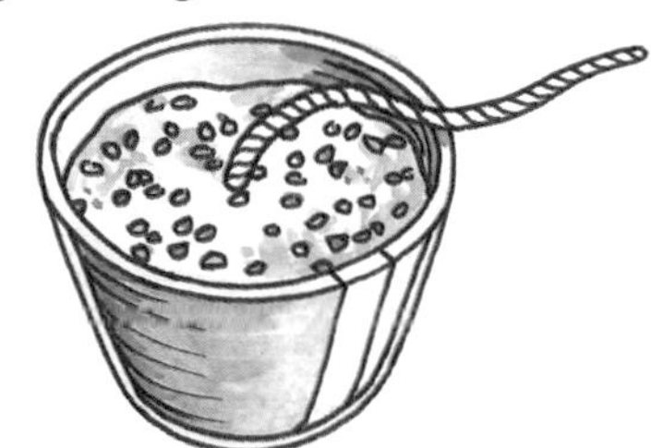

4 **Push the end of a piece of string** down through the middle of the container with a skewer. Leave the cake to cool and harden before you remove the container.

5 **Tie the cake to the branch of a tree** or the edge of a feeding station.

Broad-leaved Forest

Here you will see plenty of oaks, maples, hickories, willows, beeches, elms, cottonwood, and locusts. These trees have broad leaves and lose them in the fall. Overhead they meet to form a thick, high canopy, while small shrubs and plants grow in the deep shade on the forest floor underneath.

Many kinds of birds live here—woodpeckers, woodland hawks, thrushes, and warblers. The trees and shrubs provide a varied diet of seeds and insects and, of course, many places for the birds to roost and nest. You will have to be patient to see forest birds. Many are shy and keep themselves hidden in the leaves and shrubs. But you will definitely hear them. Learning to recognize their songs will help you to identify them.

Spring and summer are the best times to look for birds in these forests. About three-quarters of the birds that breed here migrate south for the winter. Look for some of the birds from the evergreen forest (shown between pages 56 and 65) too, as they also come to broad-leaved and mixed woods.

Where forests have been cleared, thickets—small trees, bushes, and shrubs—might grow up in their place. Look out for warblers, sparrows, and finches in thickets, and on the edge of forests. Many of these birds winter here. The picture shows ten birds from this book; how many can you recognize?

Yellow-billed Cuckoo, Rose-breasted Grosbeak, Great Horned Owl, Scarlet Tanager, Wood Thrush, Wild Turkey, Turkey Vulture, Black-&-white Warbler, Hairy Woodpecker, Red-headed Woodpecker

Wild Turkey

Family Group: Gamebird
Size: male c.46 ins; female c.37 ins
Forages in groups
Eats seeds, nuts, acorns, insects
Also found in scrub

You cannot mistake this large game bird. Its body and wings are black with white stripes. Look for the blue and red wattles on its head. The male has a large tail which it opens like a fan to attract the female. It spends most of its time foraging on the ground although it roosts in trees at night. In spring the male gobbles so loudly it can be heard up to a mile away. Females are smaller and less colorful than males. The eggs are gray, speckled with darker gray, and the female lays 8 to 15 on the ground, hidden under thick undergrowth.

Ruffed Grouse

Family Group: Gamebird
Size: 16–17 ins
Usually alone
Eats seeds, insects, berries, and plant buds
Also found in mixed woodlands

This bird goes through two color phases—red and gray. The change is most noticeable in its large tail with bands of either red or gray across it. Look for the wide dark band near the tip. Look for the small crest on its head, too. You are most likely to see a Ruffed Grouse near the edge of a forest. When it is disturbed, it bursts into flight with a roar of wings. In the spring the male tries to attract the female by beating his wings making a drumming sound. The eggs are tan and lightly speckled brown and 9 to 12 are laid in May or June in a hollow next to a tree or rock.

Great Horned Owl

This owl is big and powerful with large rounded wings. It has long ear tufts like the Long Eared Owl, but you can easily tell them apart by the Great Horned Owl's enormous size. It hunts at night and its call is a deep HOOO-HOO-HOO. Its eggs are white and the female lays 2 or 3 of them between January and April. It may use an unused nest or make its own in trees, caves, or in a sheltered place on the ground.

Family Group: Owl
Size: 21–22 ins – Hunts alone
Eats small and large prey, even including skunks and grouse
Also found in other habitats

Barred Owl

This medium-sized owl has dark rings around its eyes and face and wide stripes across its upper breast and dark streaking down its wings. It likes damp woodlands and hunts mainly at night when you might hear it clearly hooting OO-OO-OOO-OOOO. During the day it is well hidden on its roost, but, since it is easily disturbed, you may hear it hooting then too. The eggs are white and the female lays 2 or 3 between February and April, usually in a hole in a tree or in an unused nest.

Family Group: Owl
Size: 20–22 ins
Hunts alone
Eats rodents, birds and small animals
Also found in evergreen forests

Yellow-billed & Black-billed Cuckoos

Cuckoos have slim bodies and long tails with black and white bands underneath. The Yellow-billed and Black-billed Cuckoos are both brown on top and white underneath. The color of their bills, and the white tail spots of the Yellow-billed, are the best way to tell them apart. The Yellow-billed is common all over the US except in northwestern states and California. Look for the cinnamon colour in its wings as it flies. Its song is a hollow but sharp KUK-KUK-KUK. She builds a nest of twigs, but sometimes she lays her 3 or 4 greenish-blue eggs in the nest of another bird.

Family Group: Cuckoo
Size: 10–12 ins
Usually alone
Feeds mainly on caterpillars and other insects
Summer visitor

Red-headed Woodpecker

The Red-headed Woodpecker is black on top and white underneath and its whole head and throat are red. Look for the white patch on its wings and its white rump. It is found east of the Rocky Mountains in the US and Canada. You will probably hear it before you see it, drilling with its sharp beak into the bark of a tree. But you could also see it on the ground searching for food. The female lays 4 to 7 white eggs in a hole she has dug out of a tree, post, or telephone pole.

Family Group: Woodpecker
Size: 9–10 ins
Usually alone
Eats insects, nuts and berries
Also found in parks and gardens

Pileated Woodpecker

This large, black woodpecker has a red crest and white lines on its face. When it is flying look for the white under its wings. Look for the large, rectangular or oval nest holes it excavates in trees, too. Like all woodpeckers it likes to make a new nest hole every year, and so provides a constant supply of old nest holes for other kinds of bird to use. It lives in the eastern states of North America and across central and southern Canada to the West Coast. The female lays 3 to 5 white eggs.

Family Group: Woodpecker
Size: 15–17 ins
Usually alone
Eats ants and other insects in trees and stumps
Also found in parks

Yellow-bellied Sapsucker

As its name suggests, you can tell this bird by its yellow underparts. Look for the red forehead, white wing patch and white rump, too. The male has a red chin and throat. Sapsuckers drill holes in the trunk of a tree, then return later to feed on the sap and insects that have gathered in the holes. This bird breeds in forests in Canada and the northeastern US. The female lays 4 to 7 white eggs in a hole she has dug into a dead or dying tree. In the fall it migrates to the southern states and Mexico.

Family Group: Woodpecker
Size: 8–9 ins
Usually alone
Eats sap and insects
Also found in evergreen forests
Summer visitor

Family Group: Woodpecker
Size: 9–10 ins
Usually alone
Eats insects that bore into tree bark

Hairy Woodpecker

You may see this woodpecker in forests all the way across North America. Look for its white back and the white stripes on its wings. Its face is black and white with red on the back of its head. It looks similar to the Downy Woodpecker but has a larger bill. Like all woodpeckers it has short legs and claws to give it a good grip when climbing and it uses its stiff tail feathers to support itself as it cuts into a tree. The female lays 3 to 5 white eggs in a hole dug into a tree.

Family Group: Woodpecker
Size: 9–10 ins
Usually in small noisy groups
Eats acorns and nuts in winter, insects in summer

Acorn Woodpecker

You may see this noisy, sociable woodpecker in California and parts of the southern US. It is shiny black on top, white underneath with a broad black breast band and streaked belly. Look for the its red cap. Listen for its call—a harsh JA-COB. It has the unusual habit of drilling small holes in trees or poles and storing acorns in them for the winter. The female lays 4 to 6 white eggs and, unlike other woodpeckers, reuses its previous nest.

Cooper's Hawk

You may see this hawk throughout the year in the US and southern Canada. It looks like the Sharp-shinned Hawk except that it is larger and its long tail is rounded at the end, not squared. Watch it soar with fast wing beats interrupted by periods of gliding. The female lays 3 to 5 off-white eggs, lightly spotted with brown.

Family Group: Hawk
Size: 16–20 ins – Usually alone
Preys on songbirds and small mammals

Broad-winged Hawk

This hawk perches on a low branch waiting for its prey. It is brown on top with white underparts banded with rust. Look for its hooked bill and sharp talons. If it is flying you will easily see its broad white wings edged with black and its black and white banded tail. It breeds in the eastern US up to the Gulf of St Lawrence. Its call is a high-pitched whistle. It may make a badly-built nest, but will often use the old nest of a crow. The female lays 2 to 4 whitish eggs spotted with brown.

Family Group: Hawk
Size: 13–15 ins – Migrates in huge flocks
Preys on mice, frogs, snakes and some birds
Summer visitor, though a few spend the winter in southern Florida

Sharp-shinned Hawk

This hawk is gray above and chestnut below with white stripes. When it is flying, look for its long squared tail with four or five clear dark bands and for its rounded wings. Its call is a high-pitched KA-KA-KA. It breeds in Canada and parts of the northern US. Its nest is a large well-built cup of twigs, usually hidden high in an evergreen tree. The female lays 3 to 6 white eggs with brown spots. In the fall it migrates to the southern US.

Family Group: Hawk
Size: 10–14 ins
Usually alone but may migrate in loose groups
Preys on small birds, some insects, and rodents
Also found in mixed woodlands

Whip-poor-will

This bird is hard to spot but easy to hear. Its clear WHIP-POOR-WILL call gives it its name. Its overall gray-brown color camouflages it well, but look for its long rounded tail and black chin with a white "necklace." It feeds after dark, catching moths and insects as it flies. It breeds in eastern states and the Southwest. The female lays 2 white eggs spotted with gray. In the fall it migrates to the Gulf Coast and Florida.

Family Group: Nightjar
Size: 9–10 ins – Feeds alone
Eats flying insects
Also found in evergreen forests

Red-shouldered Hawk

You may see this hawk in most woodlands in eastern states and California. It is one of the easiest to see during the day. When it is soaring high in the sky, look for its large rounded wings with clear black and white bands on its flight feathers, and dark gray tail with narrow white bands, too. The rust colored "shoulders" can only be seen from above. Its call is a high-pitched KEE-AH or KAH. It nests high in a tree and lays 2 to 4 white eggs spotted with brown.

Family Group: Hawk
Size: 15–24 ins
Usually alone or in small flocks in fall
Preys on snakes, frogs, mice, crayfish, young birds

Turkey Vulture

You can tell this vulture by its bald, red head and large, hooked bill. Its talons are too weak to grab live prey, so it feeds instead on carrion and garbage. It soars and glides on its large wings which it holds in a shallow V. Look for the flight feathers which are clearly paler than the rest of the wing and the body. It breeds in the US and southern Canada. It does not make a nest, but simply lays its 2 pale yellow eggs, blotched with brown, on bare ground or cliffs.

Family Group: Vulture
Size: 26–32 ins – Often soars in loose groups
Scavenges on garbage dumps and on dead animals
Also found in many other habitats

Broad-leaved Forest

Eastern & Western Wood-Pewees

There are two kinds of Wood-Pewee that nest in North America. It's hard to tell them apart but this doesn't matter because their ranges don't overlap. Both are dull brown on top with two white bars on the wings, and whitish underneath. Listen for the PEE-A-WEE call of the Eastern bird and the PEE-ER call of the Western bird. Both birds make their nests on a horizontal branch of a tree and lay 2 to 4 white eggs, spotted with brown.

Family Group: Flycatcher
Size: 5–6 ins – Alone or in pairs
Eats flying insects – Summer visitor

Bewick's Wren

Wrens are small chunky birds with long curved bills. They are very active and curious. They can often be tempted into the open by squeaky noises. The Bewick Wren holds its long tail high above its back and wags it from side to side. It has a brown back and white underparts. Look for the white stripe over its eyes. It is more common in the western US than the East. It makes its nest in old woodpecker holes, nest boxes and other holes. The 5 to 7 white eggs are spotted with brown.

Family Group: Wren
Size: 4–5 ins – Usually alone – Eats insects

Brown Creeper

You might find this bird in most parts of North America in winter. You will probably hear its high-pitched SEE-SEE-SEE call before you see it. It is brown and tan streaked on top with white underparts. Look for it on a tree trunk, digging its long, curved bill into the bark to search out insects and larvae. It breeds in Canada, and the northeastern and western US. It usually builds its nest beneath a piece of loose bark. The female lays 4 to 8 white eggs, speckled with reddish brown.

Family Group: Creeper – Size: 5–6 ins
Usually alone, but can join flocks of titmice and nuthatches in winter
Eats insects and larvae from bark

Fox Sparrow

Family Group: Sparrow
Size: 7–8 ins
Usually in small groups
Eats mainly seeds

This sparrow varies in the color of its plumage, but always has white underparts with spots or streaks. It usually has a rusty-colored rump and tail and many have a gray crown and back. Watch it kick both feet backward as it feeds in leaf trash. It breeds in northern Canada and Alaska and southward through the Rockies. It nests on the ground under a bush where the female lays 4 or 5 white eggs washed blue or green and spotted with brown. In the winter you may see it on the Pacific coast and in the southern states.

Wood Thrush

You will see this chubby bird only in the eastern US. It is the largest of the brown and spotted thrushes. Look for its reddish brown back (especially around the head) and large dark breast spots. It sings loudly and tunefully in phrases of 3 to 5 notes. It makes its nest of grass and mud and lines it with roots. The 3 to 5 greenish blue eggs are incubated by the female alone.

Family Group: Thrush
Size: 7–8 ins
Alone or in groups
Eats insects and berries
Summer visitor
Also found in swamps and suburbs

Ovenbird

You are most likely to see this bird foraging for food on the ground. It is olive-brown above and white underneath streaked with black. Try to spot the reddish crown bordered by black stripes. Look too for its pink legs. It walks, rather than hops, with its tail cocked. It is common in eastern states and much of Canada. Its song is a loud TEACHER-TEACHER-TEACHER. It makes an oven-like nest among fallen leaves on the ground and lays 3 to 6 white eggs speckled with brown.

Family Group: Wood Warbler
Size: 5–6 ins
Usually alone
Eats insects and tiny ground animals
Summer visitor, though a few spend the winter in Florida

Veery

This bird is a typical small thrush, but you can tell it apart from others by its blurry breast spots and uniform, reddish brown coloring on top. Like other thrushes it is white underneath with a speckled breast. It is named after its song—a series of descending VEEER notes. It is a common but shy bird. Look for it in damp woodlands and thickets along the US-Canada border and the Appalachians and Rockies. It builds its nest on the ground using twigs and grass and lays 3 to 5 greenish blue eggs.

Family Group: Thrush
Size: 6–7 ins
Alone or in groups
Eats insects and berries
Summer visitor

Orchard Oriole

Orioles have long tails and pointed beaks. The male Orchard Oriole has a chestnut body and black hood, wings, and tail. Instead of chestnut, the female is greenish on top and greenish yellow underneath. You are most likely to see them in the eastern US in orchards or other areas of scattered trees. Its nest is a hammock of grasses hung from a fork in a tree, and the female lays 3 to 7 white eggs, spotted with brown. Sometimes ten or more birds may nest in the same tree.

Family Group: Oriole
Size: 7–8 ins
Usually alone or in pairs
Eats insects and berries
Also found in suburbs
Summer visitor

Black-headed Grosbeak

This large finch has a heavy triangular bill. The male has a black head, black back, tail, and wings. Look for his rich cinnamon-colored underparts. The female is brown on top with a tan, slightly streaked breast. You are most likely to see it in the western US along the edges of woodlands and in clearings. Its nest is a platform of twigs in which the female lays 3 to 5 greenish blue eggs, spotted with brown. The male has the unusual habit of singing while taking his turn to sit on the eggs.

Family Group: Bunting and Sparrow
Size: 8–9 ins
Usually alone
Eats seeds, berries and insects
Summer visitor

Rufous-sided Towhee

Family Group: Bunting and Sparrow
Size: 8–9 ins
Usually alone, or in small groups
Eats on the ground on insects and seeds

The male is black on top with flecks or patches of white. It has a black hood and white underparts. The female is brown and the male is black. Look for the long tails and chestnut sides which give this bird its name. You might see it in most of the US and southern Canada at some time of the year. Watch them scratching the ground for food with both feet together. Listen for their call. In the West it is TOW-WHEE and in the East DRINK-YOUR-TEA. They lay 3 to 6 white eggs spotted with brown.

American Redstart

This bird is easy to spot by the colorful patches on its wings and tail. The male is black with a white belly and orange-red patches. The female is olive-green with patches of yellow where the male is orange. Look for it chasing flying insects, or watch it as it perches, spreading its wings and fanning out its tail. It breeds in most of North America except for the far North and the Southwest. It nests in a tree and lays 3 to 5 white eggs speckled with brown.

Family Group: Wood Warbler
Size: 5–6 ins
Alone or in small groups
Eats flying and other insects
Summer visitor, though a few spend the winter in southern Florida

Rose-breasted Grosbeak

This chunky bird is black on top, white underneath and has a red breast. The female is brown on top and tan streaked with brown underneath. Look for the huge white bill. You are most likely to find this bird in the northeastern US and Canada, but stretching farther west in Canada. They like re-growing woodlands and waterside thickets. Its nest is a platform of twigs placed high in a tree in which the female lays 3 to 5 green-blue eggs speckled with brown.

Family Group: Bunting and Sparrow
Size: 8–9 ins
Usually alone
Eats seeds, berries and insects
Summer visitor

Scarlet Tanager

The male is one of the most beautiful birds of North American woodlands. Only the black wings and tail break up the brilliant scarlet. The female is greenish olive on top and yellowish underneath. You might hear its harsh whistling in the summer in woods in eastern states. Its nest is a loose cup of twigs and grasses built high up on the end of a tree's branches. The female lays 3 to 5 blue-green eggs, spotted with brown. It migrates to South America for the winter.

Family Group: Tanager
Size: 7–8 ins
Alone or in pairs
Eats insects and berries
Summer visitor

Prairie Warbler

Like many warblers, this bird is olive-green on top and yellow underneath. Look for the black streaks on its side and the patch of yellow surrounded by black under its eyes. In the spring and summer you may see it in thickets in the eastern US and south eastern Canada. Look for it twitching its tail as it forages in low shrubs and brush. Despite its name, it is not a prairie bird. It nests in low bushes and the female lays 3 to 5 white eggs speckled with brown.

Family Group: Wood Warbler
Size: 4–5 ins
Usually alone
Eats insects
Summer visitor, though a few spend the winter in southern Florida

Nashville Warbler

Family Group: Wood Warbler
Size: 4–5 ins
Usually alone
Eats insects
Summer visitor

You will easily spot this bird's yellow underparts. Look for the gray head and the white ring around its eyes, too. You are most likely to see it in re-growing woods and in damp spruce bogs. Listen for its SEE-WEET song. It breeds along the Canada-US border, but not in the prairies. It nests on the ground and lays 4 or 5 white eggs, spotted with reddish brown. Some birds fly to the coasts of California and south western Texas in winter, but most fly farther south.

Hooded Warbler

The male has a very clear black hood and yellow face. The female is yellow underneath and green on top, like the male, but has faint black markings only. These birds like to hide in damp woodlands so you are more likely to hear it than see it. Its song is a loud musical whistle which sounds like TA-WIT TA-WIT TA-WIT TEE-YO. It breeds in the eastern US and builds a bulky nest of leaves and grasses. The female lays 3 to 5 white eggs spotted with brown.

Family Group: Wood Warbler
Size: 5–6 ins
Usually alone
Eats insects
Summer visitor

Wilson's Warbler

Family Group: Wood Warbler
Size: 4–5 ins
Usually alone
Eats insects, often while flying
Summer visitor

This warbler was named after Alexander Wilson, a famous Scottish-American birdwatcher. It looks like the Hooded Warbler except that the male has black only on the crown of his head. The female has no black. Listen for its song—a long descending series of CHIP notes. It breeds in damp thickets in northern Canada and much of the West. It makes a large nest of leaves and grasses, well hidden on the ground. The female lays 4 to 6 white eggs speckled with brown.

Red-eyed Vireo

This bird is common in the eastern US and Canada. It is olive-brown on top and white underneath. Look for the black and white stripes over its eyes. Its red eyes are difficult to see unless you are lucky enough to get very close to it. You will certainly hear it, though, because it sings all day as it searches through the bushes for food. The female lays 3 to 4 white eggs, spotted with reddish brown. They migrate as far south as Colombia and Venezuela for the winter.

Family Group: Vireo
Size: 5–6 ins – Usually alone or in small groups
Eats insects in the summer, berries in the fall
Summer visitor

White-eyed Vireo

Although this bird is common in the eastern US, you could be lucky to get a good look at it because it likes to hide in dense thickets. It sings loudly, a scolding five- to seven-note song, beginning and ending with a sharp CHIP. If you see it, look for the two whitish wing bars on its olive-green wings. Try to get close enough to see its yellow eye glasses and white eyes. It lines its nest with lichens and spiders' webs and the female lays 3 to 5 white eggs spotted with brown.

Family Group: Vireo
Size: 4–5 ins
Usually alone
Feeds mostly on insects

Black-and-White Warbler

Family Group: Wood Warbler
Size: 5–6 ins
Alone or in loose groups
Eats insects
Summer visitor

Both males and females are boldly marked with black and white. Look particularly for the black and white stripes on the crown. Watch for them climbing up and down tree trunks and branches, like creepers do, looking for insects to eat. Listen out for its song, a series of high, thin WEE-WEE notes. It breeds in eastern states, stretching farther north and west in Canada. It hides its nest among the roots of a tree where the female lays 4 to 6 white eggs spotted with reddish brown.

Feeding Stations

The best place to start bird watching is in your own back yard. And the best way to attract birds there is to put out food and water for them. You will have no trouble enticing pigeons, starlings, and other common birds to come and feed. In fact you will probably be surprised by how many different kinds you see. However, you are more likely to get some of the smaller seed-eating birds like finches and chickadees if you make a feeding station.

Simple bird feeder

1 **Find an old plastic tray** and ask an adult to drill some holes around the edge. One at each corner plus two or three more along each edge will do.
2 **Loop some nylon cord** through the holes at each corner to hang it by. The other holes are to let rainwater drain off.
3 **Hang the feeder from the branch of a tree** as far out of the way of cats and squirrels as you can. Tie the cord firmly.

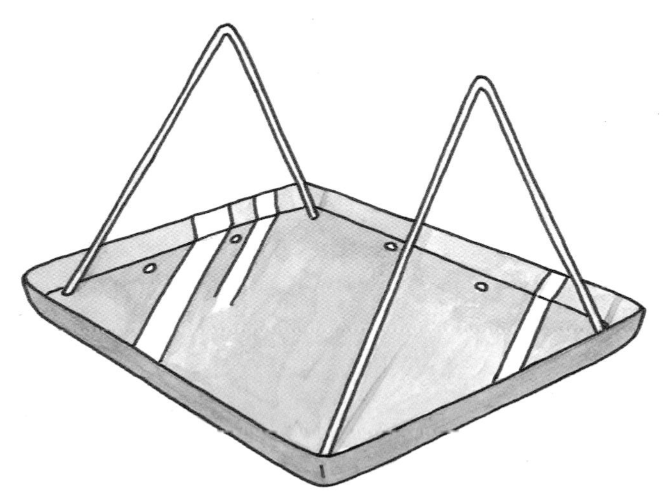

Wooden bird feeder

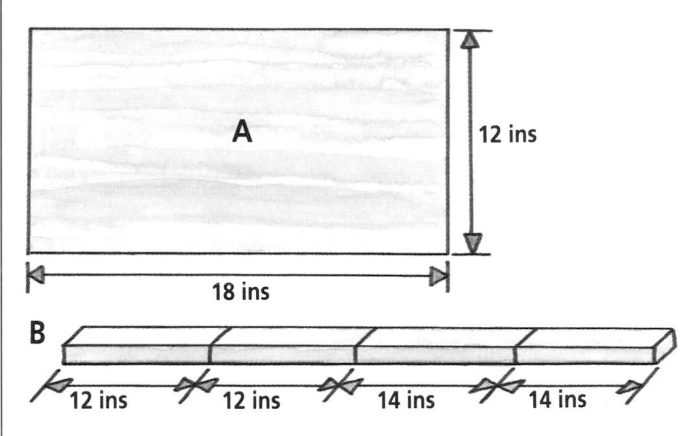

You'll need one wood rectangle about 12 x 18 ins **(A)**, a strip 4 ft 4 ins x 1 ins x 1 ins, and a 4 ft post **(C)**. If it is to go on a patio,you'll need a plank of wood measuring 9 ft x 3 ins x 1 ins.
1 **Ask an adult to help you saw the strip** into four pieces, two measuring 12 ins long, and two 14 ins long **(B)**.
2 **Coat all the pieces with wood preservative** and leave them to dry.

Water

Birds also need extra water when the ground is frozen. If it freezes too, replace it with fresh water.

At any time of the year, birds will enjoy a bird bath. You can make this quite simply from the lid of a garbage can, a large potted-plant saucer, or some other wide, shallow basin. If you make sure there is always water in it, the birds will soon know where to come for a drink or a bath.

If you use the lid of a garbage can, support it with bricks or stones on four sides. Put a heap of small stones in the middle so that the water does not get too deep for small birds.

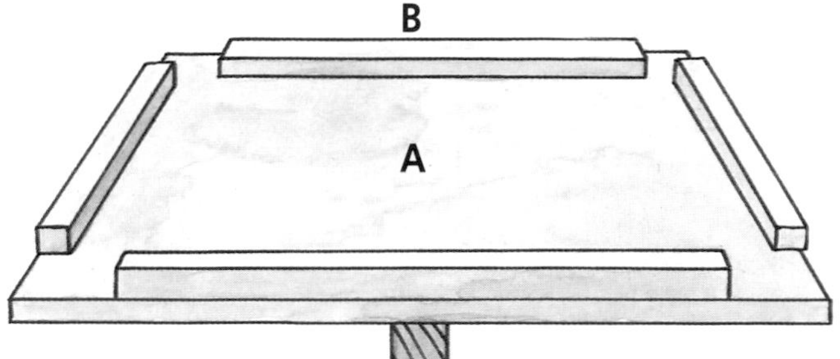

3 **Glue or nail the four strips of wood (B)** onto the rectangle **(A)** as shown. The gaps at each corner are very important because they let rainwater run off and make it easier to clean the tray.

4 **Nail the post (C)** onto the underside of the board in the center.

5 **For a patio, cut the plank into eight pieces:** four measuring 12 ins long **(D)**, plus four pieces measuring 15 ins **(E)** each.

6 **Nail the four 12 ins strips (D)** to the bottom of the post to make feet. Then nail on the four 15 ins diagonal pieces **(E)** as shown to make the feeder stand up on its own.

Where to put the feeder?

Before you decide where the feeder is to go, think about where it will be safest from cats and squirrels. Remember that both are good jumpers. Try to keep it away from shrubs, fences, and walls.

The second thing to think about is: can you see it from your house? You want to be able to watch the birds without disturbing them.

Looking after the feeder

Once you start putting out food for the birds, make sure you keep doing it. They will expect it! Wintertime when the ground is frozen and many of the trees are bare is when the birds most need extra food. Suggestions for different kinds of food are given on pages 22–23.

Before adding new food, make sure that the tray is clean. If there are bird droppings among the leftover seeds, throw them away too.

Use warm, soapy water to wash the tray, then rinse and dry it before adding new food.

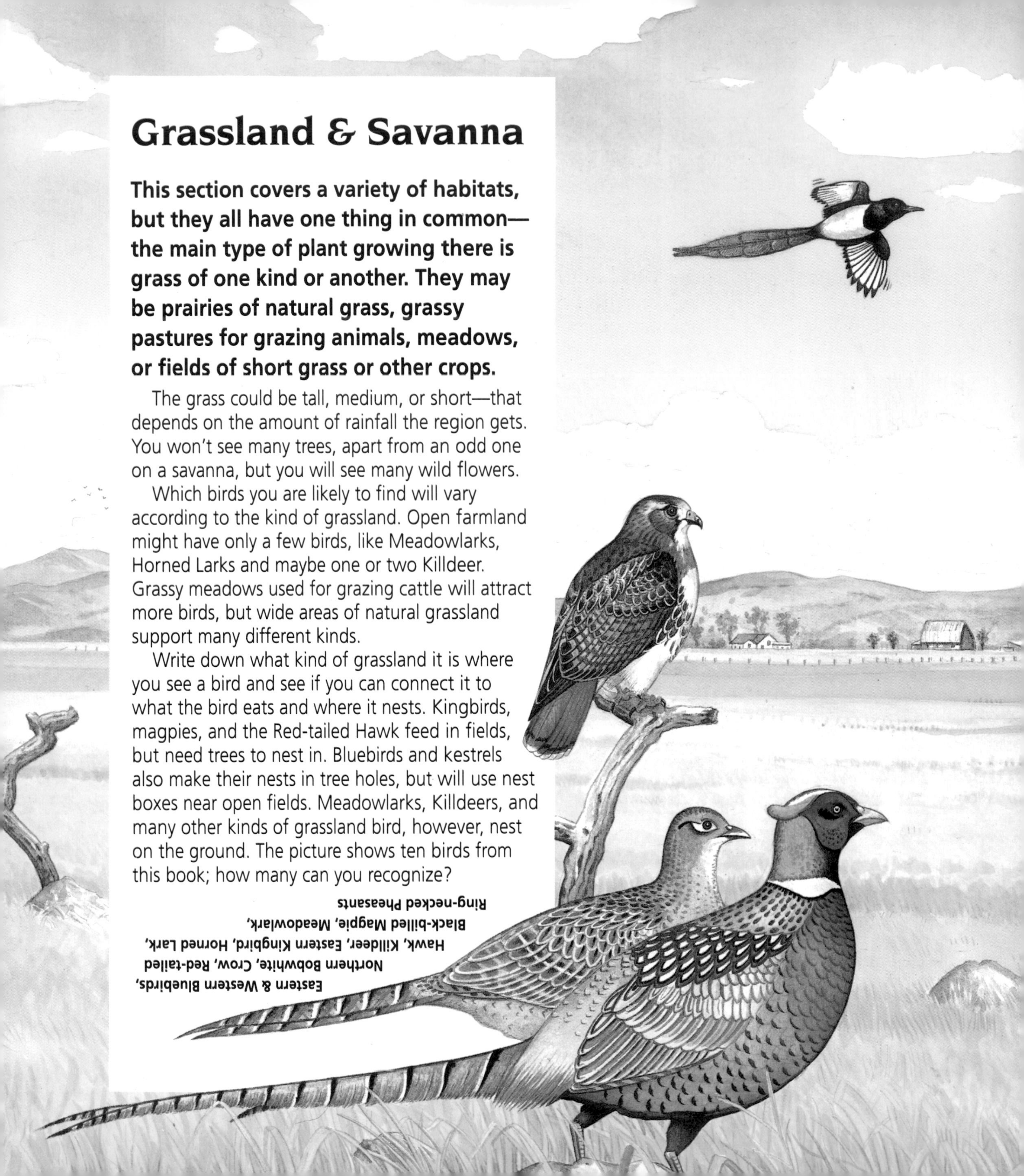

Grassland & Savanna

This section covers a variety of habitats, but they all have one thing in common—the main type of plant growing there is grass of one kind or another. They may be prairies of natural grass, grassy pastures for grazing animals, meadows, or fields of short grass or other crops.

The grass could be tall, medium, or short—that depends on the amount of rainfall the region gets. You won't see many trees, apart from an odd one on a savanna, but you will see many wild flowers.

Which birds you are likely to find will vary according to the kind of grassland. Open farmland might have only a few birds, like Meadowlarks, Horned Larks and maybe one or two Killdeer. Grassy meadows used for grazing cattle will attract more birds, but wide areas of natural grassland support many different kinds.

Write down what kind of grassland it is where you see a bird and see if you can connect it to what the bird eats and where it nests. Kingbirds, magpies, and the Red-tailed Hawk feed in fields, but need trees to nest in. Bluebirds and kestrels also make their nests in tree holes, but will use nest boxes near open fields. Meadowlarks, Killdeers, and many other kinds of grassland bird, however, nest on the ground. The picture shows ten birds from this book; how many can you recognize?

Eastern & Western Bluebirds, Northern Bobwhite, Crow, Red-tailed Hawk, Killdeer, Eastern Kingbird, Horned Lark, Black-billed Magpie, Meadowlark, Ring-necked Pheasants

Northern Harrier

This bird of prey has long, narrow wings and a long tail. Look for it flying low over the ground, its wings raised up, looking for its prey. The male bird is gray on top and white underneath, with black tips on its wings. The female is brown above and mottled tan below. Look for the white band across the rump on both the male and the female. It nests in the northern US and Canada, and flies south for the winter. The female lays 4 to 5 white eggs, a wash of blue with brown spots.

Family Group: Hawk
Size: 17–20 ins
Hunts alone
Eats mice, rats, frogs, and other prey
Also found in open fields

Loggerhead Shrike

Shrikes perch on a branch and scan the ground for prey. Then they pounce on it with their large, hooked beaks. They store their prey on thorns and barbed wire. There are two kinds of shrike in North America and they are hard to tell apart. The Loggerhead Shrike is slightly smaller and darker than the Northern Shrike, which is mainly a winter visitor. Both are gray with black wings and tail. Look for the black mask stretching across the eyes and the patch of white on the wings. The Loggerhead Shrike makes its nest in bushes and hedges and lays 4 to 6 gray-white eggs, with brown spots.

Family Group: Shrike
Size: 8–10 ins – Usually hunts alone
Preys on insects, small birds, and rodents

Red-tailed Hawk

This is one of the most common hawks. You are likely to see it on open fields near woodlands. It is brown on top and paler underneath. Look for the narrow dark band across its belly and the plain, reddish orange tail. Its wings are broad and roundish. You will easily see it circling high in the sky, waiting to pounce on its prey below with its hooked beak and sharp talons. Listen for its high-pitched distinctive KEE-ARGH call. Its nest is a heavy mass of twigs built high in a tree. The female lays 2 to 4 white eggs, speckled with brown.

Family Group: Hawk
Size: 19–25 ins
Alone or in pairs
Mostly eats mice

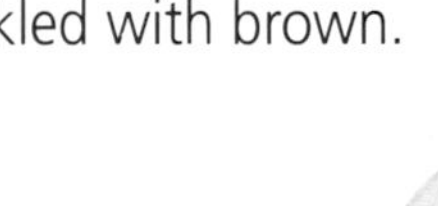

Common Nighthawk

Although nightjars feed mainly during the night and roost during the day, the Common Nighthawk also flies during the day. It is so well-camouflaged you aren't likely to see it roosting on the ground or on a branch or roof. Look for it in the air. It is dark gray and its wings are long and pointed with a bold white band across them. Its tail has a fork with a narrow white band near the end. Listen for its nasal PEENT call. It is a summer visitor to most of North America. Unlike other nightjars, it nests on roofs as well as in hollows in the ground. The female lays 2 creamy-colored, olive-buff eggs.

Family Group: Nightjar
Size: 9–10 ins
Alone or in groups
Eats flying insects, mostly moths
Also found in open woods and towns

American Kestrel

This bird of prey is our smallest falcon and is common in most of North America. You might see it in cities as well as in open country. Look for it hovering, or perched on a branch or telephone wire. It has a rusty-colored back and a long rusty-colored tail with a black band at the end. The male has dark-blue inner wings and patches of rust, black, and white on his head. The female is browner and her head has less clear markings. She makes their nest in a bare cavity in a tree or building and lays 3 to 7 white eggs, heavily spattered with reddish brown color.

Family Group: Falcon
Size: 9–11 ins
Usually on its own
Mostly eats insects in summer, small mammals in winter

Northern Bobwhite

This is really the only small gamebird that is common in the eastern US. It is brown on top and scaled white underneath. Its sides are striped with reddish brown. The male's face and eye stripe are white, the female's creamy. In the spring and summer listen for the male's distinctive BOB-WHITE whistle. It makes its nest in a dip in the ground hidden by overhanging plants, and lines it with grass. The female lays 7 to 20 white eggs.

Family Group: Quail (Gamebird)
Size: 8–11 ins
Usually feeds and roosts in coveys, except when breeding
Eats the ground on seeds, insects
Also found in open woodlands

Vesper Sparrow

This well-streaked sparrow has less obvious markings on its face than other sparrows. Look for its white eye rings, dark ear patches and chestnut along its shoulders. When it is flying, look for the white, outer tail feathers. This sparrow was called "Vesper" because it seemed to sing better in the evenings. Its song is rich and melodious. It breeds in open fields with lots of weeds and along the sides of roads. The female lays 11 to 14 eggs which she incubates alone. In the fall it migrates to the southern states.

Family Group: Sparrow
Size: 6–7 ins – Usually seen in ones or twos
Eats seeds and insects

Field Sparrow

The Field Sparrow is rustier-looking than the Vesper Sparrow and has two white bands on its wings. It has a stubby, bright-pink beak and a white ring round its eyes. Its call is a sad whistle which rolls into a trill. It breeds in the prairies, the eastern US,and southern Canada. Its nest is a cup of grasses which it makes in a low bush. The female lays 2 to 5 blue-gray eggs, spotted with brown. Some birds move south to parts of Florida and Texas for the winter.

Family Group: Sparrow
Size: 5–6 ins – Usually in seen in pairs or small flocks
Eats seeds

Killdeer

You will easily see this plover in fields and grasslands. Watch it dart across the ground, stop, then dart off again. Look for the two black bands across its breast and the black pattern on its face. If it flies off, look for its pointed tail and rusty-colored rump, too. Listen for its repetitive and piercing KILL-DEE call. Its nest is a dip lined with plants and small stones in which the female lays 4 pale tan-colored eggs with black spots. She will pretend that she has been hurt in order to chase egg-thieves away from her nest.

Family Group: Plover
Size: 9–11 ins
Alone or in pairs
Eats insects and tiny animals
Also found on freshwater and saltwater mudflats

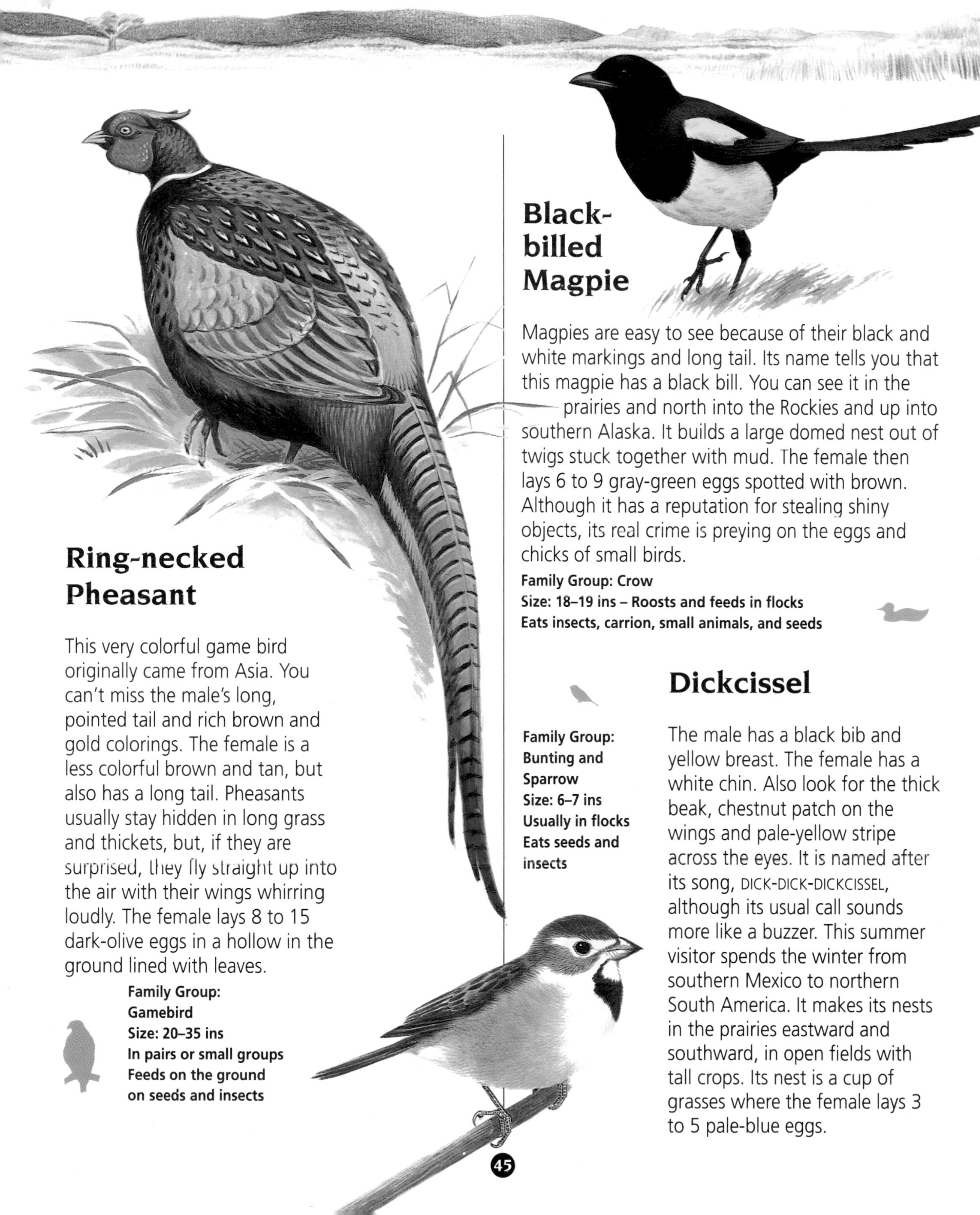

Black-billed Magpie

Magpies are easy to see because of their black and white markings and long tail. Its name tells you that this magpie has a black bill. You can see it in the prairies and north into the Rockies and up into southern Alaska. It builds a large domed nest out of twigs stuck together with mud. The female then lays 6 to 9 gray-green eggs spotted with brown. Although it has a reputation for stealing shiny objects, its real crime is preying on the eggs and chicks of small birds.

Family Group: Crow
Size: 18–19 ins – Roosts and feeds in flocks
Eats insects, carrion, small animals, and seeds

Ring-necked Pheasant

This very colorful game bird originally came from Asia. You can't miss the male's long, pointed tail and rich brown and gold colorings. The female is a less colorful brown and tan, but also has a long tail. Pheasants usually stay hidden in long grass and thickets, but, if they are surprised, they fly straight up into the air with their wings whirring loudly. The female lays 8 to 15 dark-olive eggs in a hollow in the ground lined with leaves.

Family Group: Gamebird
Size: 20–35 ins
In pairs or small groups
Feeds on the ground on seeds and insects

Dickcissel

Family Group: Bunting and Sparrow
Size: 6–7 ins
Usually in flocks
Eats seeds and insects

The male has a black bib and yellow breast. The female has a white chin. Also look for the thick beak, chestnut patch on the wings and pale-yellow stripe across the eyes. It is named after its song, DICK-DICK-DICKCISSEL, although its usual call sounds more like a buzzer. This summer visitor spends the winter from southern Mexico to northern South America. It makes its nests in the prairies eastward and southward, in open fields with tall crops. Its nest is a cup of grasses where the female lays 3 to 5 pale-blue eggs.

Bobolink

In the summer the male is black with white bands across its wings and rump and a creamy hood on the back of its neck. At other times it looks like the female—streaked with black and tan on top and tan-colored underneath. Look for their sharply pointed, tail feathers. It is named for its call, a bubbling and continuous BOB-O-LINK. In the southern states it is sometimes called the Rice Bird, because of the large quantities of seeds it eats. This summer visitor may spend the winter as far south as Brazil and Argentina. Its nest is a cup of grasses on the ground where the female lays 4 to 7 gray eggs, spotted with brown.

Family Group: Blackbird – Size: 7–8 ins
Eats seeds – Usually in groups, especially in the fall

American Goldfinch

This bird is often known as the Wild Canary because in the summer the male is yellow all over except for its black crown, wings, and tail. The female is green on top and pale yellow underneath. Look for its bounding flight and for the two white bands on their wings. In the winter the male's face and throat are yellow. His body is brownish on top; the female is grayer. Watch for this bird using its delicate beak to pick out the seeds from the head of a thistle and separate them from the fluffy parachutes. The female lays 2 to 7 blue eggs in a nest in a low tree or hedge.

Family Group: Finch
Size: 5–6 ins
Forms large groups, especially in winter
Eats seeds

Eastern & Western Kingbirds

The Western Kingbird (below right) has a yellow belly, gray head, breast and back, and black wings and tail. The Eastern Kingbird (below left) has a black crown and almost black back, wings, and tail. Its underparts are white. These birds are usually seen perching on a branch, post, or telephone wire, waiting to dart out and grab a flying insect. Eastern Kingbirds nest in most of North America except the far West and Southwest. The Western Kingbird is most common in the western US. Both build their nest of twigs and lay 3 to 5 white eggs spotted with brown.

Family Group: Tyrant Flycatcher
Size: 8–9 ins
Alone or in groups
Eats flying insects

Eastern & Western Bluebirds

Both of these birds are blue on top and rusty underneath, although the Western Bluebird is darker than the Eastern Bluebird and has a gray belly instead of a white lower one. The Western Bluebird also is chestnut on its upper back. The females are gray instead of blue on top. Look for these birds perching on twigs and branches. Watch them drop off the branches to catch insects on the ground or in the air. Listen for their calls. The Eastern Bluebird's is a melodic CHUR-LEE, the Western Bluebird's is a deep repeated FEW. Both birds build their nests in holes in trees or in nest boxes. They lay between 3 and 7 pale blue eggs.

Family Group: Thrush
Size: 6–7 ins
Usually in pairs or small groups
Eats insects and fruit

Horned Lark

This bird is brown and tan streaked on top, whitish underneath. The black "horns" are often hard to see, but the black markings on its face, neck, and crown are easy to spot. When it is flying, look for its black tail with white outer feathers. The Horned Lark likes to breed in the short grass in the prairies and the tundra. Its nest is a simple cup of grasses on the ground where the female lays 4 greenish eggs speckled with brown. In the winter you may see it in empty fields or on the shore.

Family Group: Lark
Size: 7–8 ins – Usually seen in groups
Also found on shores – Eats seeds and insects on the ground

Eastern & Western Meadowlarks

Both of these birds are streaked on top and yellow underneath. In the summer look for the V-shaped black band on the breast. These birds are not shy and you can get quite close to them. Although they look alike, they sound very different. The Eastern Meadowlark's call is a SEE-YOU-SEE-YER whistle. The Western Meadowlark's song sounds like something bubbling. Their nests are grassy cups with a domed roof, hidden in the grass. Both females lay 3 to 7 white eggs spotted with brown.

Family Group: Blackbird
Size: 9–10 ins
Usually seen in pairs or small flocks
Eats insects and seeds on the ground

When you go on a serious bird-watching expedition, you must dress properly. If it is cold, dress warmly, as you will be spending a lot of time keeping very still. Also, try to wear clothes that do not make noise as you move. Dress in quiet, dull colors that will blend in with the ground and bushes. Dull greens and browns are good. Anything bright will alert the birds. If it is snowy then, of course, white is best.

Take a notebook, pencils, eraser, this book, and binoculars with you. You will get the most out of your expedition if you keep a record of what you see. Do your best not to let the birds know you are there. Making a blind for yourself will help.

Making a blind

If you know of a good place to watch birds but can't get close enough without bothering them, then why not build your own blind?

1 **Find four wooden posts** about 5 ft long for the uprights, and four boards about 3 ft long for the top.

2 **You will also need a piece of canvas** measuring about 13 ft square to cover a blind for one person.

3 **Paint or dye it all over** with green and brown splotches to camouflage it. Leave a flap for the door and cut out two narrow slits for windows.

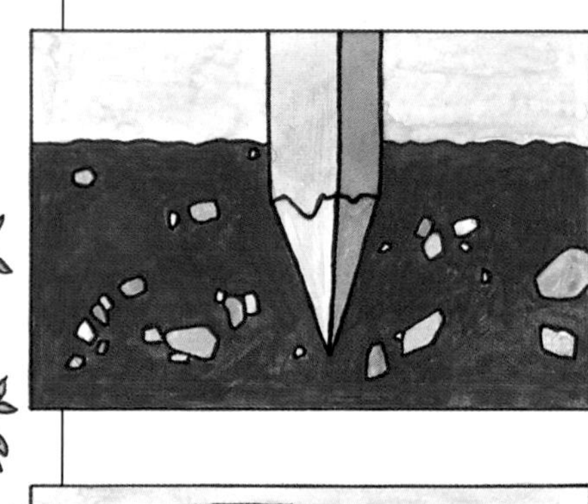

3 **To build the blind**, hammer the upright posts firmly into the ground. Ask an adult to help you with this.

4 **Tie the top boards to the posts**, as shown in the picture. Find something to sit on as well.

5 **Hang the canvas over the top**. Put some large stones around the bottom of the canvas to stop it from flapping in the wind.

6 **Leave your blind empty for a day or two** so the birds can get used to it before you use it.

7 **Once you begin using it**, you must always remain very quiet. The slightest noise will frighten off any birds you may be watching.

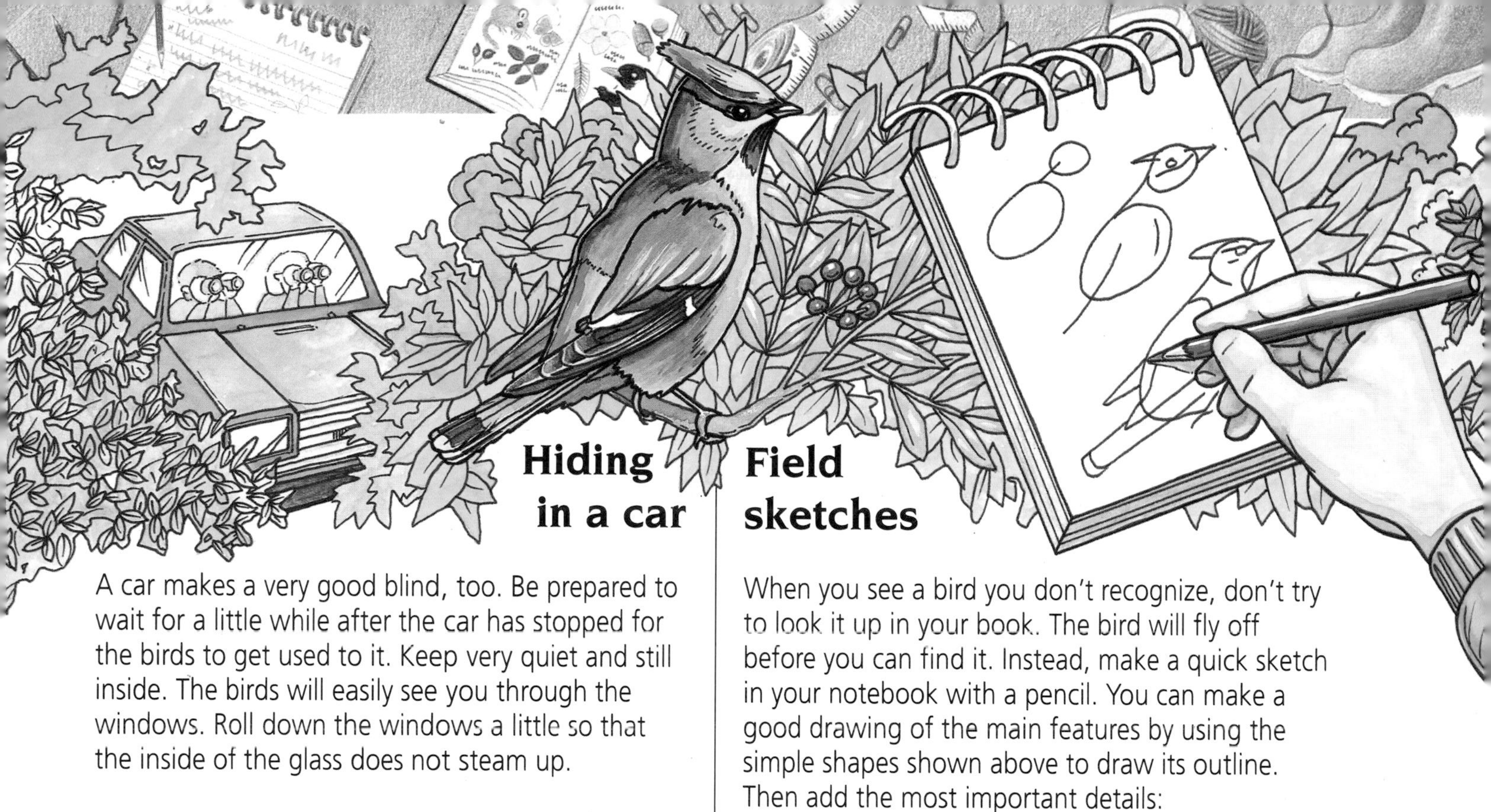

Hiding in a car

A car makes a very good blind, too. Be prepared to wait for a little while after the car has stopped for the birds to get used to it. Keep very quiet and still inside. The birds will easily see you through the windows. Roll down the windows a little so that the inside of the glass does not steam up.

Footprints in plaster

In wet weather or after a thaw, look for some clear bird footprints in the mud in your yard. You can make a cast of them.

1 **Bend some card into an oval** to make a mold.

2 **Mix up some plaster of Paris** according to the instructions on the box.

3 **Put your mold over the footprint** and pour in the plaster of Paris mixture.

4 **Let the cast harden** before you lift the mold and the plaster.

5 **Wash off the dirt** before you leave the plaster for a few days to set really hard. You can paint or varnish the footprint.

Field sketches

When you see a bird you don't recognize, don't try to look it up in your book. The bird will fly off before you can find it. Instead, make a quick sketch in your notebook with a pencil. You can make a good drawing of the main features by using the simple shapes shown above to draw its outline. Then add the most important details:

- Where are the main patches of color?
- What shape is its tail?
- Can you see the shape of its beak?

Make a note of what the bird is doing and any other information that will help you identify it. Now you can look it up in your book.

A field notebook

Use your field sketches as the basis for a field notebook. For each bird you see, write down the date, where you saw it, and what kind of habitat it was in. If you know the bird already, you can still record what it was doing, whether it was alone or in a group, and what other birds were nearby.

Desert & Mesquite

This section covers the mesquite or cactus deserts of the southwestern US, and sagebrush desert. They have little rain and are very hot in the summer. You won't be surprised to find cactus, yuccas, and other desert plants growing here.

One of the reasons that birds can survive well in deserts is because they can fly over large areas looking for water. Some have adapted extremely well—the Black-throated Sparrow lives in some of the most inhospitable deserts of the US. Others, like the Vermilion Flycatcher, keep to the scrub around ponds and streams on the edge of the deserts.

Some birds move to more fertile areas during the long hot season, but others breed and nest in the desert. They usually breed during the short rainy seasons. Then the desert blooms with wild flowers and insects, providing lots of food to feed the chicks. The picture shows eight birds from this book; how many can you recognize?

Inca Dove, Costa's Hummingbird, Elf Owl, Scaled Quail, Chihuahuan Raven, Great Roadrunner, Black-throated Sparrow, Cactus Wren

Elf Owl

This tiny owl lives in the deserts and dry woods along the Mexican border and farther south. It has a short tail and is striped and spotted with brown, tan, and chestnut. Like all owls it has a round head and its yellow eyes point forward. It is active at dawn, dusk, and through the night. !ts call is a group of high CHIRRUPS. It often nests in trees or in old woodpecker holes in cacti and lays 3 to 4 white eggs. During the day it roosts in these holes.

Family Group: Owl
Size: 5–6 ins
Usually alone
Feeds mainly on insects
Summer visitor

Chihuahuan Raven

Ravens look a lot like crows, although they are larger and their tails are wedge-shaped. But you aren't likely to find crows in the dry lands of the southwestern US where the Chihuahuan Raven lives. To be sure, listen for its call, which is a long drawn-out croak. The Chihuahuan Raven used to be called the White-necked Raven because its heavy black ruff covers a white neck. Its nest is a platform of twigs which it uses again and adds to year after year until it becomes very big. The female lays 4 to 7 olive-green eggs, spotted with brown.

Family Group: Raven
Size: 19–20 ins
Forms large flocks
Preys on insects, small animals, plus carrion and fruit

Great Roadrunner

This is another well-known bird that lives on the ground and likes running more than flying. It has a long, black tail and is heavily streaked with brown and white. It has a large, heavy, black beak and an obvious bushy crest. Look for it speeding across the desert on its long, strong legs. It builds a neat saucer-shaped nest among the thorns of a cactus plant and lays 3 to 6 white eggs. The female incubates the eggs as soon as they are laid, so the eggs do not all hatch at the same time.

Family Group: Cuckoo
Size: 22—23 ins
Usually alone or in loose groups
Eats insects, lizards, snakes, rodents and small birds

Costa's Hummingbird

You will only see this tiny bird in the waterless parts of southern California and Arizona, and many move farther south for the winter. It is green on top and white underneath. The male has a violet-colored head which may look black in weak light. You are most likely to see this bird feeding with its long, needle-like beak from a cactus flower. It hovers as it feeds, its wings beating so fast they hum. The female lays 2 white eggs in a tidy nest built across the low branch of a bush.

Family Group: Hummingbird
Size: 3–4 ins
Alone or in small groups
Eats nectar of flowers and insects

Inca Dove

Doves are the same shape as pigeons, but are smaller. The feathers of the Inca Dove form a very clear, scaly pattern above and below. Look for the chestnut coloring on its wings when it is flying and for the black and white feathers on its long, gray tail. Listen for its coo-coo call. Its nest is a platform of twigs in which the female lays 2 creamy-white eggs. Like other doves, it has a long breeding season, with at least 2 and sometimes 5 broods of young each year.

Family Group: Dove
Size: 7–8 ins – Forms flocks – Eats seeds

Scaled Quail

Quails are chubby chicken-like birds. The Scaled Quail is found only in the semi-deserts of the southwestern US. Look for its pale white-tipped crest for which it is sometimes known as "cotton-top." It is gray-brown on top and rusty underneath. Its breast and side feathers are black on the edges, making it look scaly in front. It feeds on the ground and likes to run rather than to fly. Its nest is a hollow in the ground, hidden in prickly plants, in which the female lays 9 to 16 tan eggs with brown spots.

Family Group: Quail (Gamebirds)
Size: 10–12 ins
In coveys, except when breeding
Feeds from the ground on seeds and some insects

Cactus Wren

This is our largest wren and is very noisy. Its back and wings are streaked and banded in white, black, and dark brown. Its white breast has heavy black spots. Look for its long, slightly curved beak and long tail, usually standing straight up. You are most likely to find it in cactus country. Listen for its harsh CHA-CHA-CHA which you can hear at any time of the day. Its nest looks like a haystack among the thorns of a cholla or yucca. In it the female lays 4 to 7 pinkish eggs spotted with brown.

Family Group: Wren
Size: 8–9 ins – Alone or in pairs
Eats insects, spiders and their eggs

Black-throated Sparrow

This bird lives in some of the hottest and driest deserts in North America, from Oregon and Wyoming to central Texas. It is brown on top and white underneath. It is named for the black patch on its throat. Look for the two white streaks on its face, too. It builds its nest of stems and grasses placed in a bush or cholla cactus. The female lays 3 or 4 white eggs washed with pale blue.

Family Group: Sparrow
Size: 5–6 ins
Often in small groups
Eats seeds of desert plants

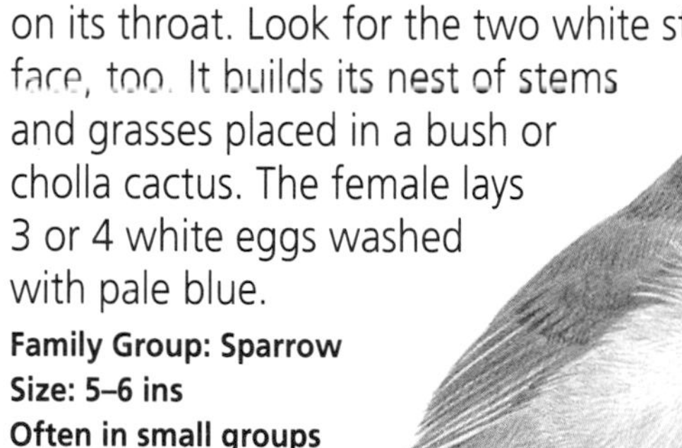

Abert's Towhee

This bird is one of a group of long-tailed ground birds—the towhees. It is brown on top and creamy-colored underneath. Look for its black face and long tail. It lives in the dry woodlands and scrub of southeastern California and Arizona. It is shy and secretive so listen for its call—a sharp PEEK—and its song, a rolling trill of PEEK notes. Its nest is a cup of stems and plants built in a low bush. The female lays 2 to 5 bluish green eggs, spotted with brown.

Family Group: Bunting
Size: 9–10 ins – Alone or in small groups
Feeds in seeds and insects on the ground
Also found in farmlands and near suburbs in the Southwest

Vermilion Flycatcher

Look for this bird where deserts meet trees and streams. The male is hard to miss with its bright red crown and underparts and brown upper parts. The female has an orange-red wash on her belly, a streaked breast and tan-brown upper parts. This bird likes bare, dry ground, but doesn't breed much farther north than the Mexican border. Listen for the male's soft PIT-A-SEE song. It builds its nest in a tree about 8 to 20 feet high and lays 2 to 4 off-white eggs spotted with brown.

Family Group: Tyrant Flycatcher
Size: 5–6 ins
Alone or in pairs
Eats flying insects

Long-distance Flyers

You may already be familiar with the comings and goings of Robins and Dark-eyed Juncos around your home, but look out for different birds in spring and fall. They may be pausing to rest or feed as they migrate (or move home) from one part of the country to another.

Flying uses a lot of energy, so they need to keep filling up with food. Some species, like the hawks, swallows, and gulls move in daylight. Most others, including the shorebirds, warblers, and orioles, move at night.

Where do they go?

Some birds have quite spectacular journeys. The Arctic Tern travels farthest, from its breeding grounds in the Arctic to spend the winter in the Antarctic. In the fall, the American Golden Plover flies from northern Canada to Argentina. Instead of keeping to the coast, it island-hops across the West Indies. But it rarely stops to rest; it can fly up to 2,000 miles without pausing.

Why do birds migrate? Many birds that breed in North America spend the winters in the warmer south. There they can escape the cold weather. Others may migrate to fresh sources of food, but no one can fully explain the regular movement of some birds in spring and fall.

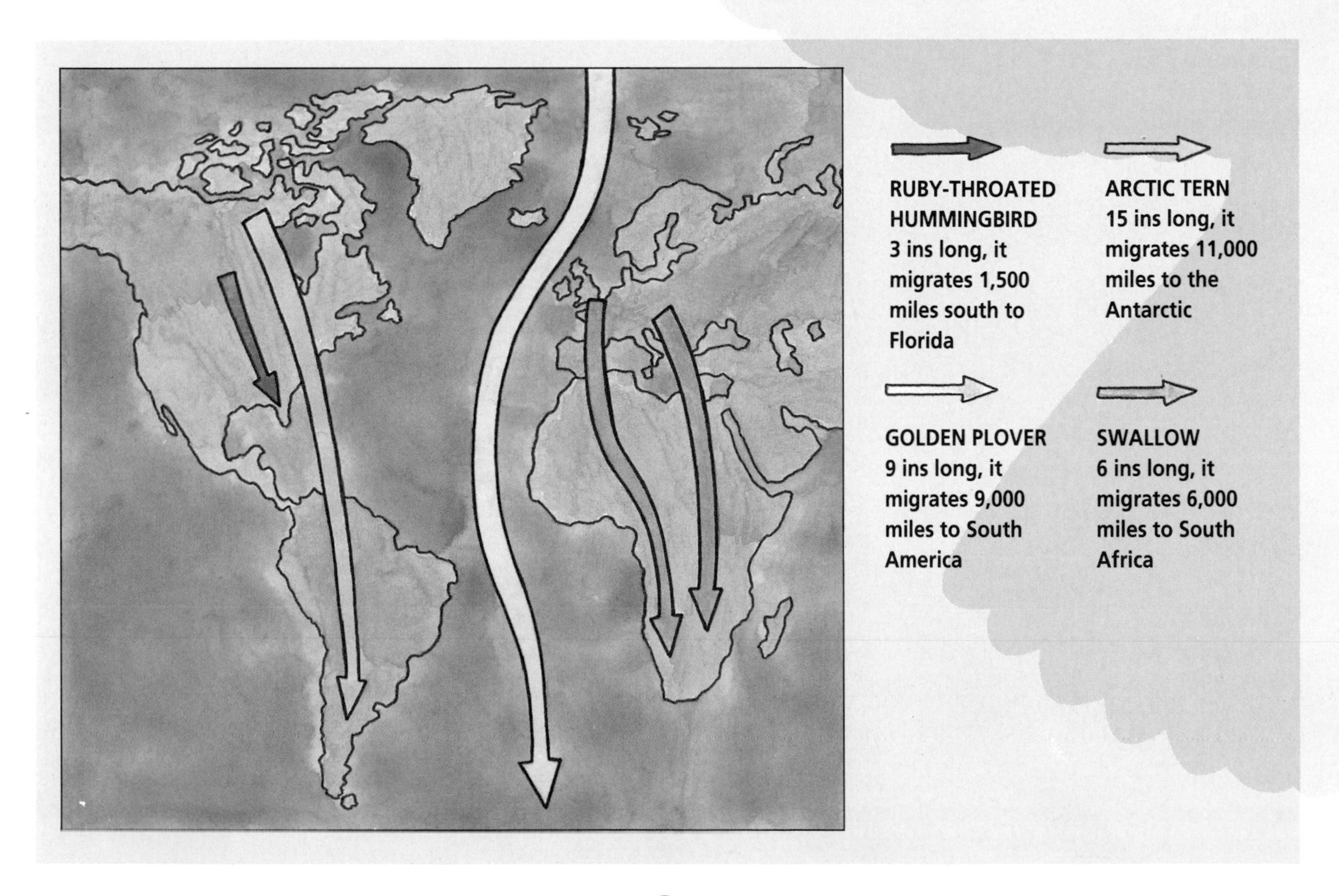

Finding their way

How birds migrate is even more mysterious, but they probably use the sun or the light of the stars to find their way. Many birds migrate up the coast. This is safer than flying across oceans and probably helps them to stay on course. But on foggy nights they may become confused by the long flashes of lighthouses and fly straight towards them. To stop birds flying into them, some lighthouses have changed to using short flashes only.

Bird warning

Migrating birds that are just passing through can be confused by large windows. They may try to fly through them and stun themselves. You can help by hanging a warning in your window. A hawk shape works well because most birds keep well away from hawks.

1. **Trace the hawk shape** on this page onto a piece of thin paper with a pencil.
2. **Glue it onto a large piece of thin card** like an old cereal packet or carton. Carefully cut around the edges with scissors.
3. **Color the hawk shape black** using a crayon or paint. The blacker you can make it, the better.
4. **Attach about 2 ft of string** to the head of the hawk with scotch tape and thumb-tack it to the top of your window frame.
5. **If you can attach it to the outside of your window**, it will move about in the wind and look more realistic. But first cover it in plastic to keep the rain off it. If you use black plastic it will save you coloring in the shape.
6. **You can also hang glittering or tinkling objects** in a problem window. Scotch-tape long streamers of tin foil to the top of the frame or hang up some wind chimes.
7. **Or you could tack some light, see-through material** over the glass to reduce the reflections. This need only be up during the danger periods in the spring and fall.

Evergreen Forest

These forests form a wide belt across northern America, called the "boreal" (or northern) forest. This habitat is also found down the Pacific coast among the Rocky Mountains. The trees you are most likely to see here are pines, spruces, hemlocks, firs, junipers, and tamarack. All these trees are coniferous, which means that they produce cones containing seeds and they mostly have needles for their leaves.

Evergreen forests also grow in a band high up in the mountains. In these places the summers are usually cool and the winters very cold. Many birds come to these forests to breed, then fly south to spend the winter in warmer places. You may find some of the same birds in broad-leaved forests and on evergreen trees in mixed woodlands, too.

Many small birds live in the evergreen forests. They feed on seeds and insects and roost and nest in the trees. Grosbeaks and finches have strong, sturdy beaks which they use to pick out the seeds from fir cones. Crossbills have special crossed beaks for picking out the seeds of pine cones.

You will hear many fine songs in these forests, from warblers and thrushes in particular. Learning to recognize their songs will help you identify them. The picture shows seven birds from this book; how many can you recognize?

Red Crossbill, Pine Grosbeak, Spruce Grouse, Pine Siskin, Western Tanager, Hermit Thrush, Yellow-rumped Warbler

Pine Gosbeak

Family Group: Finch
Size: 9–10 ins
Alone or in small groups
Eats seeds
Also found in other habitats, even suburban yards in winter

You can tell this is a finch by its chunky beak and the way it flies up and down, rather than straight from one perch to another. The male is red all over except for his long black tail and wings. Look for the two white bands on the wings. The female is a warm buff-orange on the head, but is gray where the male is red. You might see this bird in the North of Canada and farther south in the East and West into the US. The female lays 4 or 5 blue-green eggs spotted with brown.

Red Crossbill

In the spring and summer you are most likely to see this bird in the forests of Canada and the western mountains, but in the winter you might see it almost anywhere. The male is red with brownish wings and tail. The female is greenish yellow instead of red. It can bc hard to see its crossed beak, which it uses to pick the seeds out of pine cones. When it is flying, look for its short, notched tail and listen for its clear JIP call. It makes its nests nearly all year and lays 3 to 5 blue eggs spotted with brown.

Family Group: Finch
Size: 6–7 ins
Alone or in small groups
Eats pine seeds and insects
Also found in other habitats

White-winged Crossbill

This bird is similar to the Red Crossbill except that it has two bold white bands on its wings. Look for the crossed beak and short notched tail, too. When it is flying you might hear its CHET-CHET call. It is most common in the evergreen forests of Canada and the northern Rockies, but it and the Red Crossbill (see opposite) can show up almost anywhere where there are pine cones. It can breed almost all the year round and lays 3 or 4 pale green eggs spotted with brown.

Family Group: Finch
Size: 6–7 ins – Alone or in small groups
Eats pine seeds and insects
Also found in other habitats, especially in winter

Pine Siskin

In most of the US you will see this bird only in the winter. Most fly north to Canada to breed, although some stay in the western mountains all year. It is streaked brown and black on top and brown and white underneath. It has a thin beak for a finch. When it is flying, look for the yellow on its wings. It makes its nest of twigs and grass and decorates it with lichen. The female lays 3 to 6 blue eggs spotted with brown. Although it always nests in evergreen trees, it often visits other trees, particularly alders.

Family Group: Finch
Size: 4–5 ins
Usually in flocks
Eats seeds

Pine Warbler

You can tell this warbler is different from the finches by its longer tail and beak and its pleasant trilling song. It is olive-green on top and yellow underneath. It has two white bands on its olive-green wings. You might see it in pine woods in the eastern states. Watch for it crawling along the branches and trunks of pine trees, searching in the bark for insects. Its nest is a cup of grasses and stems lined with pine needles in which the female lays 3 to 5 white eggs spotted with brown.

Family Group: Wood Warbler
Size: 5–6 ins
Usually alone
Eats insects, seeds and berries

Magnolia Warbler

This bird has a gray head, yellow underparts streaked with black and black wings and tail. Look for the yellow rump and white bands on the wings and the white patches on the tail. The male has a black eye mask. It breeds across Canada and southward into the Appalachians. It makes its nests in young spruce and fir trees and lays 3 to 5 white eggs speckled with brown. It always migrates across the eastern states to spend the winter in Central America.

Family Group: Wood Warbler
Size: 5–6 ins
Usually alone
Eats insects
Summer visitor

Western Tanager

You are most likely to see this stunning bird in the spring or summer in the high forests of the western mountains. It is yellow underneath with a black back, tail and wings. Look for the male's bright-red head and the two yellow bands on its wings as it flies. Its song is a harsh whistle. It builds its nest of twigs and grasses in an evergreen tree and lines it with hair. The female lays 3 to 5 pale blue eggs with light brown spots.

Family Group: Tanager
Size: 7–8 ins
Usually alone
Eats insects and berries
Also found in other habitats
Summer visitor

Hermit Thrush

This tiny thrush is brown on top with a rust-red tail and white underneath with brown and gray spots. It spends most of its time on the ground searching in plants for food, but it likes to sing from the top of a tall tree. Listen for its famous flute-like phrases. It breeds in woods across Canada and the Rockies, then migrates to the southern US and Atlantic states for the winter. It makes its nest among roots on the ground and lays 3 to 4 greenish blue eggs.

Family Group: Thrush
Size: 6–7 ins
Usually alone
Eats insects
Also found in mixed woodlands

Yellow-rumped Warbler

Family Group:
Wood Warbler
Size: 5–6 ins
Alone or in groups
Eats insects
Also found in
mixed woodlands

This bird is gray on top, streaked with black and white underneath with a black breast band. Look for the yellow patches on the rump and side. The male also has a yellow crown and some have a yellow throat. You might see this bird in many kinds of woodlands in the North and West in the spring and summer and in the South and East in the winter. It builds its nest out of twigs and grasses in pine trees and the female lays 4 or 5 white eggs which are spotted with brown.

Evening Grosbeak

This finch is easy to see. It is noisy, large, and stocky with a huge pale beak. The male is yellow with a black tail and black and white markings on its wings. The female is a grayer color. In the spring and summer it breeds in Canada and southward into the Rockies. It builds its nests in an evergreen tree and lays 3 to 5 greenish blue eggs with brown spots. It spends the winter in much of the rest of the US where large flocks will come to birdfeeders to eat sunflower seeds.

Family Group:
Finch
Size: 7–9 ins
May form large
flocks in winter
Eats seeds
Also found in
mixed woods

Spruce Grouse

You may see this chubby gamebird along the sides of roads or perched in trees in forests from Alaska to Nova Scotia. The male is easy to see with his black fan tail. Look for his black throat and breast bordered with white. You might be lucky and see him trying to attract a female. He spreads his tail, lifts the red wattles above his eyes, and beats his wings. Their nest is a hollow in the ground under a small tree. The female lays 7 to 10 deep cream colored eggs spotted with brown.

Family Group: Grouse
Size: 15–17 ins
Usually in groups
Feeds on the ground on seeds and insects

Spotted Owl

Family Group: Owl
Size: 17–18 ins
Hunts alone
Eats rodents and other small animals

This owl is brown with white spots on top and underneath. It hunts at night and so is hard to see in the daytime. Listen for flocks of small songbirds mobbing it as it roosts during the day. Look for owl pellets on the ground. The Spotted Owl is becoming scarcer as the wooded gullies and damp forests where it lives in the West and Southwest are destroyed. It usually makes its nest in a hole in a tree or cliff, but sometimes uses a hawk's old nest. The female lays 2 or 3 white eggs.

Golden-crowned Kinglet

This tiny chubby bird is greenish on top and whitish underneath. Look for the orange-red crown in the male and yellow crown in the female. Watch it nervously twitch its wings. They like to eat high up in trees so listen for their high thin SEE-SEE-SEE notes. They breed in evergreen forests in Canada, the western mountains and parts of the northern US. It builds its nest of moss and feathers and lays 5 to 10 white eggs spotted with brown. It migrates to all parts of the US for the winter.

Family Group: Kinglet – Size: 3–4 ins
Usually in ones or twos – Eats insects

Ruby-crowned Kinglet

This tiny bird also nervously twitches its wings and looks a lot like the Golden-crowned Kinglet except that its face doesn't have that bird's white and black stripes. The male has a red crest but this might be hard to see. Like the Golden-crowned Kinglet the best way to find it is by its thin, high-pitched SEE-SEE-SEE call or its typical DIDIT. It breeds in Canada and in the Rockies. Its nest is a ball of mosses held together with cobwebs and usually built high in an evergreen tree. The female lays 5 to 11 white eggs spotted with brown.

Family Group: Thrush
Size: 4–5 ins
Often in small groups
Eats insects and some berries

Red-breasted Nuthatch

This little short-tailed bird is rust-colored underneath and gray on top. Look for the black cap and black stripe through its eyes. You may find it in evergreen forests in a lot of North America, but in most of the US you will only see it in the winter. Watch it climb up, down, and around tree trunks and branches looking for food. Listen for its call—a high-pitched TOOT. It makes a hole in a rotting tree stump where it builds its nest and lays 4 to 7 white eggs spotted with reddish brown.

Family Group: Nuthatch
Size: 4–5 ins
Often in flocks especially in winter
Eats insects

Helping Birds in Danger

The best way to help endangered species is to join a wildlife group that is working to save them. They need your money and they need as many people as possible to become aware of the problems. You can do your bit as well by explaining the problems to other people.

Get involved

Find out whether there is a local group involved in wildlife conservation. If you join them, you can help with fund-raising and other local activities.

1 **Listen out for particular issues**. Is there an area of land important to wildlife which is being threatened by building work? As towns or cities grow, woods may be cut down and marshes drained to make more land for building on. You can write to senators and local government officials asking them to help your cause.

2 **Visit as many bird sanctuaries as possible.** You can not only enjoy seeing the birds but you will also see what is being done to help them.

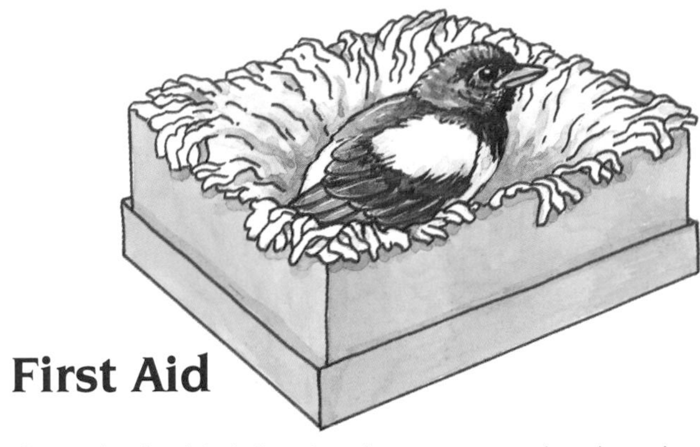

First Aid

If you find a bird that has been stunned or hurt by flying into a window, take it indoors and place it in a medium-sized box with a lid. Don't handle it any more than you have to. After a few hours' rest, it will probably have recovered enough for you to let it go. For more serious injuries, call the local wildlife society, refuge or conservation officer for advice.

If you find a chick helpless on the ground, but alive, what should you do?

1 **Don't touch it** until you have watched and listened to check whether the parents are nearby, looking after the chick from a distance.

2 **When you are sure they are not, then make a nest for the bird** in a small box with shredded kitchen towels or tissues. Keep it very quiet. Then call the local wildlife society or conservation officer to ask what to do.

Rescuing an oiled bird

A particular danger for sea birds is oil, either spilt by accident or emptied by tankers into the sea. Once a bird's feathers are covered in oil, it cannot swim or fly, so it cannot catch food and will soon starve to death. Even a small amount of oil can do a lot of harm. If the bird tries to clean itself by preening, it may swallow enough oil to kill it.

If you find a live bird covered in oil, do not try to clean it yourself. Contact a local bird group or vet who will know who can deal with it.

Keeping track

Scientists try to keep track of migrating birds by watching them on radar and also by putting an aluminum or plastic band around one leg. The band does not hurt the bird in any way.

1 **Take the band off its leg**, if you find a dead bird that has been banded.
2 **Mail the band** to the address given on it.
3 **Enclose a note** about when, where, and how you found the dead bird.

A bird-friendly garden

You can make your own small bird sanctuary in your garden with your parents' help.

1 **Ask if you can plant the trees and shrubs** that birds particularly like. Elder, dogwood, hawthorn, cotoneaster, and holly are good ones to begin with. Any tree or shrub with fruit or berries will soon bring birds into your garden.
2 **Ask if you can make a special corner** where you can let the weeds grow. Bristle grass, panic grass, and even ragweed all have seeds that birds like to eat. Sweet-smelling shrubs will attract insects—and insect-eating birds.
3 **Marigolds will attract birds** if their flower heads are left to go to seed in fall and winter.
4 **Watch carefully yourself**. What plants do the birds visit most? Which ones do they ignore? You will know which ones to keep next year!
5 **If you plant thick vines**, like honeysuckle and ivy, you may find birds nesting in them too.

Seashores & Marshes

Seashore habitats include sandy beaches, rocky beaches, and sea cliffs. Many birds come inland to breed on the salt marshes behind the shores.

Some of these birds, like the Common Tern, you will mainly see flying over the sea, but they land on the shore to roost and nest. Others feed on the beach creatures or, like Herring Gulls, on garbage.

Salt marshes form behind the seashore where rivers meet the sea and plants begin to grow. When the tide goes out, it may uncover large areas of mud flat. Few kinds of plants grow in these brackish waters, but many birds flourish here. Ducks and geese come here from inland waters, and shorebirds find shelter here too. In fall and winter, look for migrating birds, like swallows, thrushes, warblers, and hawks. The picture shows seven birds from this book; how many can you recognize?

Herring Gull, Laughing Gull, Brown Pelican, Semi-palmated Plover, Sanderling, Common Tern, Ruddy Turnstone

Common Tern

Terns have longer wings than gulls and are more delicate. The Common Tern is pale gray on top and lighter gray underneath. The top of its head is black and it has an orange-red bill with a black tip. Its legs are orange-red, too. Listen for its low drawn-out KEE-ARR call. You are most likely to see it on the coast as it migrates from its breeding grounds in southern Canada and the northeastern US coast. Its nest is a hollow into which the female lays 2 to 4 buff-olive eggs speckled with brown.

Family Group: Tern
Size: 12–14 ins
Usually in groups
Dives for fish
Migrates to South America in the winter

Herring Gull

This is the standard sea gull. Adult Herring Gulls are white with gray backs. Their gray wings have black tips. Look for its pink legs and the red spot on its yellow bill. Young birds are mottled brown. Herring Gulls get along very well with people. They scavenge whatever they can from garbage dumps and along the shore. You will easily hear their loud KYOW-KYOW calls. Herring Gulls nest inland and along the coasts across Alaska, most of Canada, and the eastern US. Each female lays 2 or 3 pale green eggs, spattered with brown.

Family Group: Gull – Size: 21–24 ins
Usually found in large groups – Eats fish and scavenges

Laughing Gull

You can see this gull anywhere along the East Coast south of Maine. It has a large red bill, black legs, and dark-gray wings with large black edges. When it is breeding it has a black head, but in the winter this fades to a dark patch at the back of the head and around the eyes. Its call sounds like a low chuckle or laugh. It nests on salt marshes. Its nest is a hollow lined with grass in which the female lays 3 olive-brown eggs, spotted with brown. Both birds incubate the eggs.

Family Group: Gull
Size: 14–16 ins – Eats fish
Usually found in flocks

Also found inland

Ring-billed Gull

This gull looks a lot like the Herring Gull, but is a little bit smaller. You can tell them apart by the color of their legs and their bills. The Ring-billed Gull has yellow legs and a black vertical stripe on its bill. You are mostly likely to see it on marshes and lakes in the summer and along the coast with Herring Gulls in the winter. It nests on islands in inland lakes and the sea. Its nest is a pile of grasses in which the female lays 3 tan-colored eggs spotted with brown.

Family Group: Gull
Size: 17–19 ins
Found in large groups
Eats fish and scavenges

Brown Pelican

Pelicans are easy to recognize because of their huge bills and pouches. The adult Brown Pelican is silvery-brown with a large, dark-brown bill and pouch. Look at the color of its neck. When it is chestnut at the back the bird is breeding or feeding chicks. Young birds are brown and whitish with dark upper parts. This is the only pelican which dives into the water for its food. Its nest is a big heap of sticks in which the female lays 2 or 3 white eggs.

Family Group: Pelican – Size: 45–54 ins
Usually found in groups – Eats fish

Red-throated Loon

The Red-throated Loon is the smallest kind of loon and it usually holds its bill pointed upwards. You are most likely to see it on the coasts in the winter when its face is white and its back is spotted with white. Loons dive under the water from the surface and are excellent swimmers. They migrate to the Far North to breed. Then they come on to land and nest close to the water's edge. They lay 2 olive-brown eggs speckled with brown or black.

Family Group: Loon
Size: 21–23 ins
Often in loose groups
Dives for fish

Willet

The Willet is large, chubby, and easy to see. Like all sandpipers, it has a long bill and long legs. It is gray and white in the winter and has heavy bands and streaks in the summer. Look for the black and white bands on its wings when it flies. It is a noisy bird, its call sometimes sounds like PEE-WEE-WEE, sometimes like PILL-WILL-WILLET. It nests on marshes and inland lakes, and lays 4 buff-olive eggs spotted with brown. It moves to the coast for the winter.

Family Group: Sandpiper
Size: 14–17 ins
Forms small flocks in the winter
Feeds in shallow water on small animals

Ruddy Turnstone

This chunky bird has a short bill and short red legs. Its wings and back are black and chestnut in the summer and grayish in the winter. Look for the pattern of white and color on its back and wings when it flies. It feeds by turning over shells and stones with its bill looking for food underneath. It nests in the Far North, laying 4 olive-green eggs blotched with brown. In the fall it flies south, and can be seen along almost every coastline in the world all through the year.

Family Group: Turnstone
Size: 8–10 ins
Often in small or loose flocks
Eats small animals on the shore

Semipalmated Plover

Plovers dart across the ground, stop suddenly, then dart off again. They have short beaks and long legs. Several kinds of plovers are brown or tan on top and white underneath with black and white head and breast markings. You should look carefully at these markings to tell this plover apart from the others. Listen for its CHUR-LEE call. It nests in the northern tundra, where the female lays 4 buff eggs spotted with brown. In the fall it migrates south along the coasts.

Family Group: Plover
Size: 6–8 ins
Often found in small, loose groups
Eats tiny animals from the surface of the wet sand or mud

Sanderling

Look for this little bird in the winter along all North American coasts. It is then pale gray, paler than any other sandpiper. Its bill and legs are black. In the summer it has a chestnut head, back and breast. You are most likely to see flocks of Sanderling running up and down the beach, keeping just in front of the surf and looking for tiny marine animals left behind by the waves. It nests in the far north, laying 4 olive-green eggs spotted with brown.

Family Group: Sandpiper
Size: 7–9 ins
Usually in small flocks
Eats mollusks and shellfish

Lakes, Rivers, & Marsh

These habitats all have open stretches of fresh water, often with shallower water round the edges with many water plants, shrubs, and trees growing nearby.

Diving birds, like the Common Merganser, use their webbed feet to swim in the open water and dive down deep for their food. Dabbling ducks, such as American Widgeon, swim too, but feed on the surface. They strain the water through their large flat bills and often "up-end" to search the water just below the surface.

Long-legged birds like herons wade in the shallow water round the edge. Then they pounce on fish with their long beaks. The picture shows seven birds from this book; how many can you recognize?

Wood Duck, Great Blue Heron, Belted Kingfisher, Common Loon, Common Merganser, Osprey, American Widgeon

Greater Yellowlegs

This bird is named after its long yellow legs. It looks gray on top, although it is really spotted black and white. It is white underneath, with some streaks on its neck and breast. Its call is a loud, descending KEU-KEU-KEU. Its nest is a well-lined scrape in which the female lays 4 buff eggs spotted with brown. In the fall it flies south and is a regular sight on salt marshes, mudflats, and lakes.

Family Group: Sandpiper
Size: 12–15 ins – Found singly or in loose flocks
Feeds in shallow water – Also found in freshwater marshes

Lesser Yellowlegs

This bird looks a lot like the Greater Yellowlegs except that it is smaller, more elegant, and its bill is shorter. Both birds are gray on top and white underneath. When they fly, you can see their white rumps behind their gray wings. The Lesser Yellowlegs even sounds like the larger bird, but its YOO-YOO call is softer and shorter. The Lesser Yellowlegs nests on the ground in Canada's evergreen forests, usually in clearings. The female lays 4 buff eggs, spotted with brown. In the fall it migrates as far south as South America.

Family Group: Sandpiper
Size: 9–11 ins – Found singly or in flocks
Feeds in shallow water – Also found in freshwater marshes

Great Egret

Family Group: Heron
Size: 35–41 ins
Often in loose groups
Eats fish
Also found in saltwater marshes

You can tell this is a heron by its long dark legs and long yellow bill. Look for the distinctive way it kinks its neck when it is resting. It is the largest white heron species and the most common worldwide. It was once hunted for its plumes. It nests in thickets and reeds on the edge of marshes. Its nest is a platform of sticks built in a tree or among the reeds. The female lays 3 to 5 pale blue eggs. It flies to the warmer southern coasts for the winter.

Snowy Egret

Family Group: Heron
Size: 20–27 ins
Often in loose flocks
Eats small mud creatures
Also found in freshwater marshes

Herons have long legs and long necks. They fly with their necks tucked in, unlike storks which stretch theirs out. The Snowy Egret is thin and elegant with white feathers. Look for its black bill, black legs, and yellow feet, although its feet could look black if covered with mud. When it is breeding, it has a crest of plumes, which made it prized by hunters long ago. Now this bird is conserved. Its nest is a platform of twigs in a tree or tall bush next to a marsh. The female lays 3 to 6 pale blue eggs.

Marshes & Wetlands

Great Blue Heron

This is our largest heron. It is mainly gray with a white head and black crest. You might see it wading on its long legs by the sides of lakes or marshes, darting out to grab a fish in its dagger-like bill. Or you may see it preening itself with its comb-like middle claw. When it flies, it tucks its neck back into its shoulders. It makes its nest of twigs near the top of a tree, returning and adding to the same nest year after year. The female lays 3 to 7 pale-green eggs.

Family Group:
Heron
Size: 39–52 ins
Alone or in loose groups
Feeds in shallow water for fish and frogs

Tundra Swan

Three kinds of swan live in North America. You can tell them apart by the color of their bills. The Tundra Swan has a black bill and there is usually a small spot of yellow in front of the eyes. When it rests it holds its long neck straight up from its breast. It makes its nest in marshes in the far north of Canada and Alaska and in the fall it moves south to ponds and lakes near the US coasts. It makes a nest of grass and moss near the water and lays 3 to 5 creamy-white eggs.

Family Group:
Swan
Size: 47–58 ins
Forms flocks in winter and on migration
Feeds in water on aquatic plants and small crustaceans

Canada Goose

Family Group:
Goose
Size: 22–36 ins
Found in flocks
Feeds in water and grazes on grassland

This is North America's most common goose. It varies a lot in size, and is easy to spot with its black head and neck broken up by a white band under its chin. It is a noisy bird and honks loudly, particularly when it is flying. Look for the large dark wings and the white stripes on the chin and rump. It nests in the north, even on ponds in city parks. The female lays 4 to 6 white eggs. In the fall look for flocks flying in a V-shape as they migrate south.

Black-crowned Night-Heron

As you can tell by its name, this heron has a black crown and eats mainly at night. It usually spends the day roosting motionless in a tree. It has a black back, grey wings and white underparts. It hunches its short neck up so you can't see it. It nests in marshes and wetlands in much of the United States and southern Canada, but moves to the coasts in the winter. It builds a substantial nest of sticks high up in a tree. The female lays 3 to 8 pale blue eggs.

Family Group: Heron
Size: 23–28 ins
May be found in loose groups
Eats fish, frogs and crustaceans

Clapper Rail

Family Group: Rail
Size: 14–16 ins
Solitary and secretive
Eats small aquatic animals

Rails have short tails and short, rounded wings. The Clapper Rail is large and pale. Its upper parts are gray-brown and its underparts have bands of gray and white. It has a long yellowy bill and pinkish legs. You are more likely to hear a rail than see it. The Clapper Rail has a loud raucous KEK-KEK-KEK-KEK call which it mainly uses at dawn and dusk. The female lays 8 to 11 cream-colored eggs, lightly spotted with red-brown. Both the male and the female incubate the eggs.

Double-crested Cormorant

Although this large, black bird has a double crest, as you can tell from its name, it is very hard to see. Look for its long, sharp bill and orange face instead. It flies with its neck stretched out. This is the only cormorant that regularly comes to freshwater lakes as well as the sea coast. Look for it spreading out its wings to dry them off after a long time fishing underwater. It nests high up a cliff or in a tree. The female then lays 2 to 7 green blue eggs.

Family Group: Cormorant
Size: 30–36 ins – Usually singly or in small flocks
Dives for fish – Also found on sea coasts

Green-backed Heron

Although this bird is a heron, it has short legs and a short neck and looks more like a bittern. Look for the chestnut face, neck and breast, and dark green back and wings. It has a black crest which it raises when it is alarmed. It likes the thick vegetation around marshes and lakes, so you are most likely to see it flying from one patch of cover to another. Its nest is a platform of twigs hidden in a bush. The female lays 3 to 5 greenish blue eggs.

Family Group: Heron
Size: 15–22 ins
Usually found alone
Eats fish
Also found in other wetlands

Pied-billed Grebe

This is one of the less colorful grebes. It is brown on top and white at the rear. In the summer, look for the black patch on its throat and the black band near the edge of its bill. In the winter, its throat and bill are both a whitish color. You aren't likely to see grebes on land. The Pied-billed Grebe even builds its nest on water. This is a floating mass of water plants in which the female lays 5 to 7 white eggs, with splashes of blue or green.

Family Group: Grebe
Size: 12–15 ins – Usually in pairs
Dives in open water for small fish and water beetles

Wood Duck

This is one of the most beautiful ducks in the world. It gets its name because it lives in woods near ponds or rivers. The female is mottled brown and spotted gray underneath. Wood Ducks have sharp claws and sometimes perch on branches or stumps of trees. They build their nests in a hollow or hole in a tree and lay 8 to 15 creamy eggs. After the ducklings hatch, they use their sharp claws to climb out of the nest. Some Wood Ducks migrate to the Gulf Coast for the winter.

Family Group: Duck
Size: 17–20 ins
Usually found in pairs
Feeds in woodland streams and ponds

American Wigeon

You are most likely to see this duck grazing in fields and marshes in large flocks. It used to be called "baldpate" after the male's white forehead. The female is grayish brown. When they are flying, look for the white patches on their wings. They breed in Alaska, Canada, and the northern states of the US. They nest in the grasses beside lakes and marshes and lay 7 to 12 creamy eggs. In the fall they migrate across the US to the coast and southern states, where you could see thousands of birds flocked together.

Family Group: Duck
Size: 17–19 ins – Forms large flocks
Dabbles in water for food & grazes in fields
Also found on coasts in the winter

American Coot

This bird is black all over except for a splash of white at the front and back, because of its bill and the white outer feathers of its undertail. It spends most of its time swimming but you might also see it running over the water to escape from danger, or to take off into the air. It likes the open water but builds its nests in the cover around the edge of the water. Its nest is a bulky cup of plants into which the female lays 6 to 9 buff eggs spotted with black.

Family Group: Rail
Size: 14–15 ins
Forms large flocks in the winter
Dives for water plants

Family Group: Duck
Size: 21–25 ins
Usually in groups
Dabbles in the water for plants, seeds and snails

Mallard

This is our most common and familiar duck. The male Mallard is easy to recognize by its bottle-green head, yellow bill, and brown throat with a white ring around its neck. The female is mottled brown with an orange bill Look for the flash of blue on the wings, seen when they fly. Like other dabbling ducks, mallards often "up-end" when they feed, so that only their tails can be seen above the water. The nest is a hollow in the ground lined with down. The female lays 8 to 12 white eggs.

Common Loon

This bird looks a lot like a duck, but it is easy to recognize by its black head and bill and boldly checkered black and white back. In the winter this loon's back is barred with gray. It spends the winter on the West and East Coasts but moves north to northern lakes to breed. Listen for its eerie cries. Usually only one pair nest on a lake, although larger lakes may have two or more pairs. Its nest is a mass of vegetation near the edge of the water. The female lays 2 olive-green eggs with brown spots.

Family Group: Loon
Size: 27–32 ins – Usually in pairs
Dives for fish
Also found on coasts in winter

Common Merganser

This thin duck has a long thin bill with a serrated edge like a saw, which it uses to catch food. The male is black on top and white underneath with a bottle-green head. Look for the rounded crest at the back of his head. The female has a reddish head and gray body. In the winter you might see them in most of the US. In the spring they fly north to breed in northern Canada and in the northeastern US. They nest in holes in trees, among rocks, or in thick plants. The female lays 8 to 11 creamy eggs.

Family Group: Duck
Size: 22–27 ins – Usually in groups
Dives for fish and water creatures

Bald Eagle

This magnificent bird is easy to recognize by its white head and neck, large yellow bill, and white tail, but it can only be seen in remote areas. It is the symbol of the United States and nearly became extinct because of shooting and pesticides. Their numbers have recently increased, but you can only see large flocks of these birds on the coasts of Alaska and British Colombia. It makes its nest of sticks at the top of a large tree and the female lays 1 to 3 white eggs.

Family Group: Hawk
Size: 30–43 ins – Usually hunts alone
Eats fish – Also seen on sea coasts

Osprey

This lightly-built bird of prey is gray-brown on top and white underneath. Its wings are long and very narrow. When it flies, it arches them like a gull. Look for the patch of black at the bend of the wing. Watch it dive headlong toward the water, then plunge feet first to pluck a fish out of the water. It breeds in much of North America and moves south to the southern coasts for the winter. Its nest is a huge mound of twigs built on top of a tree. The female lays 2 to 4 creamy eggs heavily spotted with brown.

Family Group: Hawk – Size: 21–25 ins
Hunts alone – Eats fish

Belted Kingfisher

Only the female kingfisher has a chestnut band around her breast. The male has one blue-gray breast band only. This kingfisher is common in most of North America. Listen for its loud rattle. Look for it hovering over a pond, river, or stream before diving in head first for fish. Both male and female kingfishers use their heavy bills and strong feet to dig a long nest tunnel into a steep bank of earth, often on the side of a river or stream. The female then lays 5 to 8 white eggs.

Family Group: Kingfisher
Size: 12–13 ins
Usually on its own or in pairs
Dives for fish

Tree Swallow

Swallows have slender bodies with long, pointed wings. The Tree Swallow is metallic blue on top and white underneath. You are most likely to see them in the air, flapping their wings and then gliding—twisting and turning to catch insects. Look for them in woods near water. They build their nests in holes in trees, which they line with grass and feathers. The females lay 4 to 6 white eggs. In the fall thousands of birds flock together to migrate south.

Family Group: Swallow – Size: 5–6 ins
Usually seen in flocks – Eats flying insects

Red-winged Blackbird

The male is glossy black with red patches bordered with buff-yellow on its wings. The female is streaked black and white on top and underneath and may have a suggestion of red on her wings. In early spring look for the males preening themselves near the marshes trying to attract a mate. Listen for its KOUK-LA-REE call. The female builds a nest in the dense growth around the marsh. Then she lays 3 to 5 blue-green eggs spotted with brown.

Family Group: Blackbird
Size: 8–10 ins
Forms huge flocks in the winter
Eats seeds and insects
Also found on other kinds of wetland

Spotted Sandpiper

In the summer this bird is brown on top and white underneath with regular black spots. In the winter its underparts are white only. On the ground it bobs and teeters as it walks along. In the air it flies low with stiff jerky wing-beats. Listen for its call—a series of high-pitched WEET-WEET notes. The Spotted Sandpiper nests almost everywhere in North America, except in the Southern states. It makes its nest in a dip in the ground and lays 4 tan eggs spotted with brown. In the winter it migrates to Central and South America .

Family Group: Sandpiper
Size: 7–8 ins

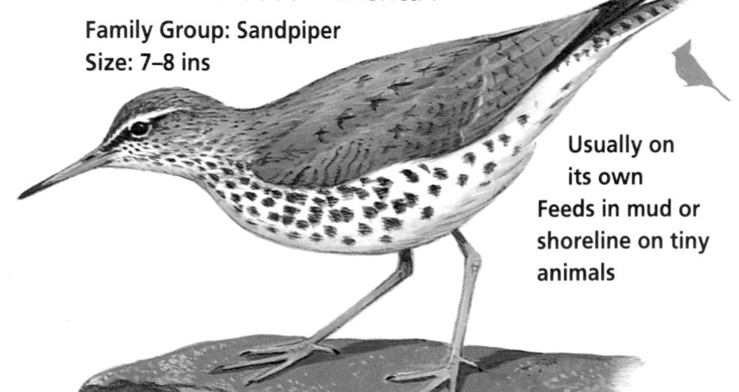

Usually on its own
Feeds in mud or shoreline on tiny animals

Marsh Wren

Wrens have slender, slightly curved bills and short tails which often stand straight up over their backs. The Marsh Wren is a rich, rusty-brown with white streaks on its brownish black back and a white stripe over its eyes. It usually stays quiet and hidden among the reeds but sometimes perches on a cattail to sing. Listen for its distinctive rattle. It builds a large nest with a side entrance almost 12 inches above the water and woven into tall reeds. The female lays 5 or 6 brownish eggs, spotted with dark brown. It migrates to southern and coastal states for the winter.

Family Group: Wren
Size: 4–5 ins
Feed on small insects and their eggs
Secretive

Find Out Some More

Useful Organizations

In addition to the national groups listed below, there are hundreds of local birding clubs and natural history associations. Check with your teacher, or with your nearest natural history museum, wildlife refuge, or local public library for information on them.

The **American Birding Association** is the largest all-birding organization in North America, and publishes a bimonthly magazine, *Birding*, along with a monthly newsletter, *Winging It*. Write to: American Birding Association, Box 6599, Colorado Springs, CO 80934: (800) 634–7736.

The **National Audubon Society** is most often associated with birds, but in recent years has taken a more general stand on environmental issues. Write to: National Audubon Society, 700 Broadway, New York. NY 10003: (212) 979–3000.

There are also independent **Audubon Societies** in the states of Connecticut, Florida, Hawaii, Illinois, Indiana, Maine, Massachusetts, Michigan, New Hampshire, New Jersey, and Rhode Island, and a central Atlantic chapter based in Maryland.

In Canada, the **Canadian Nature Foundation** is a good starting point. Write to: Canadian Nature Foundation, 453 Sussex Drive, Ottawa. Ontario K1N 6Z4; (613) 238–6154

The world-famous **Cornell University Laboratory of Ornithology** accepts associate members, and allows them the chance to take part in a number of cooperative research ventures, Including Project FeederWatch. Members also receive the lab's magazine, *Living Bird Quarterly.* Write to: Cornell Laboratory of Ornithology, 159 Sapsucker Woods Road, Ithaca, NY 14850: (607) 254–2400

Places To Visit

Because birds fly, they are often found in surprising places. Even city parks can be good places for bird-watching, especially during the spring and fall migration. Central Park in New York City, for instance, is famous for its excellent birding.

In the **East**, some of the best birding spots are along the coast. Try Acadia National Park in Maine; Jamaica Bay Wildlife Refuge in Brooklyn and Queens, New York; the Cape May Peninsula in New Jersey; Chincoteague National Wildlife Refuge in Virginia, and Corkscrew Swamp and Everglades National Park in Florida.

In the **center** of the country, Upper Souris National Wildlife Refuge in North Dakota is superb for waterbirds of all sorts, as are Valentine National Wildlife Refuge in Nebraska and Horicon National Wildlife Refuge in Wisconsin.

The **Texas** coast is among the world's great birding locations, especially during the migration season. Padre Island National Seashore, Aransas National Wildlife Refuge (winter home to the whooping crane) and Santa Ana National Wildlife Refuge are good bets there.

In the **Rockies and Southwest**, try Red Rock Lakes National Wildlife Refuge and Glacier National Park in Montana, Yellowstone National Park in Wyoming, and in Arizona, the Chiricahua Mountains, especially Cave Creek Canyon for tropical birds like trogons.

On the **West Coast** the birding can be spectacular at Point Reyes National Seashore in California for seabirds, Yosemite National Park for mountain species, and the Klamath Basin national wildlife refuges in southern Oregon and northern California for migrating waterfowl.

Index & Glossary

To find the name of a bird in this index, search under its family name. So, to look up Cactus Wren, look under Wren, not under Cactus.

Useful Books

There are probably more books on birds on than any other part of natural history. As well as the general books listed here, there are many that deal with the birds of specific states and regions; ask your library.

A Field Guide to the Birds (two volumes, East and West), Roger Tory Peterson (Houghton Mifflin Co., 1980) The most popular field guide ever.

A Field Guide to the Birds of North America, (National Geographic Society, 1983) Designed for more advanced birders, includes many rarities.

The Audubon Society Encyclopedia of North American Birds, John K. Terres (Alfred A. Knopf 1980) Huge, comprehensive reference work, but written in easy-to-read language.

Bird Finding East of the Mississippi and *Bird Finding West of the Mississippi*, Olin C. Pettingill (Oxford University Press, 1977 & 1981) The best places in every state are listed, with detailed directions.

Index & Glossary